UNCOVERED

BY

GRANITE

@ 2020 Granite

Uncovered by Granite

Published by Granite

Formatted by Living My Rhapsody

Cover by Living My Rhapsody

Cover photo by Granite

**"Envy" poem added with permission from Living My Rhapsody, and written specifically for and as part of collaboration on Seven Deadly Sins poems.

ISBN-13: 978-0-5787327-4-9

ISBN-10: 0-5787327-4-9

I am Granite

I have few talents.
I am good with stone,
chiseling away,
understanding the layers of people.
I am hard as stone;
also fragile, and can break at any moment.
So many compositions.
I can make the most beautiful piece of art,
but it can be destroyed with a single touch.
Granite is like glass,
you have to hold it just right;
one wrong angle or degree,
and it can be shattered quickly.
My fabrication of words sings a point.
I am trying to create,
but destruction is inevitable.

Little Feet,

My children are my World.

I have fought so many battles; won most, but also have lost some.

Still fighting, I hope that my babies grow to be bigger Persons than I am.

I love you guys with all my heart.

You amaze me every day.

To My Person,

There are no words in a book filled with words that can describe what
you mean to me.

I have tried.

So many of my thoughts since we met have been about you.

This very book, Uncovered, is raw and, like us, is full of passion.

All these writings are inspired by you.

You are my Guardian Angel and my Angel of Death.

"Love" is too small a word to express the way I feel about you.

Uncovered

This book has no cover.
The words are written boldly, easily recognizable, easily judged.
These words are usually misunderstood.
The emotions appear and disappear faster than the ink dries.
Some of this dye stains like a tattoo, embedded deeply into my skin.
I can't erase these pages. They are here to stay.
It took me a long time to mold this clay.
These pages are bound.
The honesty on these pages is profound.
I've hidden my words for most of my life.
This book I am writing isn't all about me,
but I write it for me.
I don't mind you digesting this novel;
that's what it's here for.
Maybe someone else can read me
and see some of these words as their own,
as the feelings that come to the surface;
or maybe some letters can be formed into their own words.
I have been misread my whole life,
but by putting these words onto these pages,
at least I'm controlling the narrative.
As misunderstood as I am,
at least now I am starting to understand myself.
I've been a part of many stories;
most don't have happy endings.
But even those stories are beautiful.
Keep reading.
I hope you get something from this book.

Astral Travel

If I could go back and change something, I think I might change my words, the way I speak, the way I show myself to people. Maybe, I should pretend to be someone I am not... but that is not me.

I am an open book.

Uncovered.

What you hear, and what you see, is what you get.

...So no, on second thought, I wouldn't change anything,

because if I went back and changed things,

I wouldn't be who I am today.

IMPACT

Wild Child

You have always been a brewing storm, a wild child.

A storm that never breaks but is completely broken.

A sky that will never be blue; it can be, but you are the son that has to rise, dry all the rain and clear the sky.

You choose to dance in lightning and are deafened by the thunder.

But when most people run for cover, you keep dancing.

You are the son I know you can be and the father I know you are.

You are stronger than the storm but choose to drown in it.

My belief, is that your lack of faith in yourself keeps the clouds rolling in.

Son, you are always there when people need you most but are never there for yourself.

Have faith son, if you are never there for yourself, one day you won't be there at all.

New Orleans (Home)

I'm from New Orleans,
the land of devils and fiends.
Walking the streets,
feeling the heat;
the air is thick, viscous.
Your brother's a dealer, best friend's a trick.
You're a jester, juggling a life of trials.
There's no one to dial, you're alone.
We're just like any other city,
but just a bit more filthy.
Living a life of guilt.
Trust is in a recession.
Life is full of depression.
This confession is honest as I can be.
If you look through my eyes,
there's a mess you don't want to see.
Stacked from floor to ceiling,
all these feelings are piled a mile high.
If I died tomorrow, I wouldn't be surprised.
I don't follow trends, I have no label,
but my life is far from stable.
The shoes I travel in aren't bigger than my brothers',
but I trip on my laces just like any other.
We all need a brace to keep us steady.
My life is torn into confetti,
sprinkled across my Home.
Everyone sees it, but no one is ready.

Mother

I lost control again today.

I'm not learning lessons of yesterday.

You've done the best a Mom could.

If I could be stronger then I would.

I still have dreams that can be achieved.

You've overcome a lot with your deeds.

But my sand is running low

and I have nothing to show.

It hurts to see you in the state you're in;

body gone and mind wearing thin.

I miss the Mom that took me to her breast.

I hope we both find peace and rest.

Father

You have always lifted me, even though I was so heavy.
Always there to lend an ear; you always had the right words,
even though I am deaf, and never heard you.
You showed me how to be a Dad.
I'm just a fraction of you, I wish I could be more.
I always said, "If I could be a quarter of the man you are,
I would have accomplished the biggest goal of my life."
You are the best role-model a person could have.
I wish I could have walked in your footsteps,
but the shoes are too big for me,
and the man you are, my Father,
is too big of a man for anyone to be.

Dale

You are the constant positive in my life.

As of writing this, almost forty years and we have never had one argument. I could stop talking to you for a decade, pick up the phone, and we will begin where we left off. I could kill your cat... not that one, but the one you like, and we would make a kitty gumbo and share a bowl. I could take a shit on the front seat of your car and you would sit in it and give me a ride.

Friend, family, again words falling short in a book of words. I guess the best way to describe you is being a piece of shit.

Dale, go fuck yourself!

Icewind Dale

Stay focused, don't let your mind wonder,

as it does for everyone.

Don't occupy your thoughts with darkness.

Keep your mind focused on the good things.

Distance can be hard to deal with.

Set goals and focus on them.

Look forward to these moments.

Remember you have to look after yourself first.

You have to take care of you before you can worry about anyone else.

Gotta love yourself before you can love others.

These words are true.

I may be the dumbest person you have ever known, but this is a fact:

"I am Dale Hoffmann Jr., the biggest waste of space."

MIA

I see you out on the streets,
defeated and starving.
I see you out in the heat,
selling your soul to make ends meet.
I tried to help you, give you a shout out,
but you're too addicted to self-doubt.
Thirsty in your self-induced drought.
Selfish.
The rain is pouring, just open your mouth.
Stop putting your hand out,
you might get bit.
Your kids need you, and that's real shit.
I'm not the best father,
but I show up,
love my kids, hope to be here when they grow up.
But time is fading,
life passes you by.
There's no time for bullshit, tomorrow you might die.
Live life to the fullest,
make every experience new.
Believe in yourself.
Always stay true.

Hey Brother

Hey brother...

I'm thinking of you today.

I wonder...what would you have to say?

Who would you be?

Would you still be Sober?

It's been twenty years since you took your life.

You were dying and wanted to go out your way.

I wonder who your daughter is today?

I wonder.

Hey brother...

We heard the angels singing that night.

It was beautiful.

All the voices carried.

I wish you were with us, but now you will never be.

I miss your smile, your laughter, so infectious.

You brought light to every dark room.

You were dying and wanted to be free.

I wonder what kind of father you would be?

I wonder.

Hey brother.

Hey friend.

Hey.

Ángel de la Muerte

You are my Angel,
a guardian, showing me love like I've never felt.
Your kisses are soft feathers but can be aggressively beautiful.
Your arms can be tender yet surprisingly strong.
What we have, just feels right.
There is nothing I've experienced
greater than you holding me tight.
Your skin is as soft as clouds.
You are my Heaven.
I don't have to die to visit these Gates;
golden in the sunlight, silver in the dark,
always shining sparkles of fascination.
No matter if my light goes dim,
I can always see you there.
But soon those feathered wings will turn black,
become coarse, and you will guide me to my stone.
I've always had bad fortune, but I am lucky to have you.
Eres mi Ángel de la Muerte.

Road Trip

This song is universal,
a voice we all hear,
music we all suffer from,
something that breaks us down,
a sad verse we can't recover from.
Life is a road trip, and the radio is playing random songs.
Sometimes we get lost and can't be found.
The music I hear is all beautiful;
the happy songs, the sad ones.
The music that is nostalgic,
the song that plays again,
and reminds us of a time,
a place where we were happy or down;
a reminder of who we are,
where we came from and what we have been through.
It's a long road, but there is always an end.

LITTLE FEET

Alexis

The hole in my heart.
I miss you beyond words.
My decision made you disappear.
It wasn't easy to make, but I had no choice.
It's a hole that can't be filled.
You are my daughter,
my child, now grown.
I miss all those years.
Believe me when I tell you,
there were many tears.
I would trade any moment from my life
to spend a minute with you.
Any moment.
I have never needed something so much.
Just a minute, that's all I ask.

Samantha

I'm not sure what you see
every time you look at me.
I see a lot of unanswered questions;
there are so many thoughts you won't mention.
So many things happened that I didn't see.
I wonder why you couldn't come to me.
I guess I can answer that myself,
I was so lost and wasn't well.
I can make all the excuses I want,
but I wasn't there, I was always on the hunt.
Always trying to satisfy cravings I had,
I wasn't there to be your dad.
Only there in body but not in mind,
I did just the expected things at the time.
I'm glad you still call when you are down;
you know I'm here and always around.
You may not need me as much as you did,
when you were just a little kid.
You will always be my World;
I love you so much, Ponygirl.

Kaleb

I remember when you were just a babe,
a little boy I needed to save.
When you were trapped in that room,
no one knew what to do.
The doctors had no idea.
I was petrified with fear.
That was the longest month of my life;
I was losing the battle, I had to win the fight.
You fought long and hard.
You conquered it all, but it left you with scars,
even those you managed to cure.
You are an inspiration and that's for sure.
Your age says you are just a child,
but the man you are makes me smile.
I wish I could be more like you;
I have a lot of learning to do.

Stay Gold

Stay bright Ponyboy and keep shining,
because every night has a silver lining.
Keep singing the songs you love to sing,
strike a chord and let the note ring.
The heart is a fine instrument to play.
Say all the things you want to say.
Life is a blink, a flash, and soon it can crash;
a match can be lit, life can turn to ash.
Keep writing choruses of laughter,
because when the lights go out, there is nothing after.
So stay golden, my Ponyboy;
keep smiling and savor all the joy.

Winter Rose

My Winter Rose,
you come in so many colors...
pastel pinks, greenish white,
deeper colors like plum and purple.
You thrive in the morning sun,
but also the shade,
dappled light.
You look so fragile,
but your strength is inspiring.
You make any day brighter.
Even when the clouds roll in,
when the sky begins to cry,
you soak it all in,
sprout your sharpest thorn
and charge into the day,
fearless.
You are the most beautiful flower in my garden.
It's a delight to watch you bloom.

Bully

Yes, I am different.

Yes, my mind doesn't think the way yours does,

because I am me and you are you.

But why do you think that gives you the right to try and take my

happiness away,

to treat me differently than the other people you know?

Maybe you are jealous that I know who I am.

Maybe other people are mistreating you.

I'm sorry if things are hard for you,

but do not take that out on me.

When I see you, I will say "hi."

You can say whatever you want to me,

but I will not let you take my joy away.

I will treat you the way I want to be treated,

I will stay positive.

I will be me... and I love who I am.

My Hearts

My loves, my heart,
you all control the flow.
My first valve was difficult.
The blockage was new.
I didn't let her free,
I tried to control her.
The second I feared.
He is a mirror.
I see myself in him.
That scares me.
I don't want him to flow in my direction.
The third is my noose.
She is my butterfly,
free and happy, but she falls quickly.
It's hard to see her not fly.
She can make my heart stop.
The fourth, she makes my heart beat.
She makes me think of time that's missed.
My heart lets me know my first is free.
My heart lets me know he needs his space.
My heart lets me know my third needs more.
She doesn't know which direction she flows.
My heart knows that all of you are a part of me.

POEMS

Sunder

Why is it raining ashes?
A hail of fire.
Why are we burning?
Crumbling, searing flakes,
building, collecting.
A mountain of destruction,
self-destructing,
melting everything down.
Showers of flames.
We should be building, constructing,
living as one, not tearing the world asunder.
Sometimes a match is lit
and a forest is burnt to the ground;
continues to spread,
rapidly running like a lake of fire.
But a seed is all it takes.
A tree of hope.
I wish to see that tree grow tall and strong.
Just one is all it takes
to start planting a forest;
but it takes a community
to keep that Eden alive and growing.

Anarchy

This beast was devastating,
swept through like the plague.
The real evil was the degeneration
of mankind.
Primal instincts took over.
Everyone for themselves.
Peoples' deepest demons rushing to the surface,
grabbing the sinners and innocent alike,
dragging them under,
stealing their souls and innocence.
I miss Home.
A wanderer.
I can't seem to find comfort.
Everything and everyone's lost,
including myself.
This was more like a wash in sewage
than a cleansing.
This natural disaster brought out the real nature of people.
The good and the evil.

Pretender

You pretend,

but I know you.

You descend,

but I see you.

I know what you want,

I know what you came for.

You think I'm transparent,

but I see right through you.

I'm the one who lets you in.

I show what I am.

You can't handle it.

There are no barriers between us,

just your blindness.

I'm more free than you will ever be.

I see your anger, I see the red.

The bloodstains will be on the innocent.

My Granite is impenetrable.

Chisel at your will; my rock is still.

You haven't even chipped this stone.

Come Home

Just a fling.
But we could have been so much more.
Honesty was my satisfaction, your body and love were just a gratuity.
The truth that came from your lips
was everything I wanted to hear.
You could have had anyone but you chose me,
even if it was just a moment in time.
If you came back tomorrow, I would be there,
waiting... arms out, ready to embrace you.
I will live my life, but I will always love you.

House of Cards*

Your last hand is the same as the first.

A hand of all black suits.

It's a dark game you continue to play.

I'm done; this game is over.

Can you accept this loss?

I understand who you are.

I can see the 'tells' in your poker face.

The evil that plagues your mind is contagious.

I admit, I was infected.

The venom that runs through your veins is as black as death.

But I found the antidote

and have freed myself from your constricting grip.

You should fold; this game can't be won.

Stop gambling with my full house of hearts.

Stay away from me and mine.

Everyone who has tried to show you love

you have pushed away.

I see no advantage to your gambit.

Just sacrifice.

It must be a lonely game.

Every time I've shown you my hand,

all I get back is a feeling of hatred and unacceptance.

I truly hope the best for you and that your luck changes.

(* Inspired by a writing from JD the Dragon)

Memorial

To the soldiers who fought,
lived, were wounded, or died.
To all the families that cry...
We lift a cup, a mug, a glass,
to all the soldiers who passed.
The price that our freedom cost.
To many lives that were lost.
Cheers to people who serve and served.
We live life free, have our words heard.
A Nation built by a strange ideal,
that our Nation is free,
and no one should kneel.
We give thanks to the fallen;
they still stand tall and steady.
The pillars that make anything possible.
To live life free, nothing is impossible.

One of Twenty-Two

One of twenty-two.

One... seems like a small sum, but that One is a big number.

It is One father,

One husband,

One soldier,

One brother,

One friend,

One son.

To you, he was everything.

A battalion, a million people wrapped in One, who fought for you,

your family, and our country.

Everyday.

Many battles that were fought and won.

Unfortunately, the war was lost.

I do not know you, and I have never met Him,

but I am told he was an amazing person.

Empire

I love the way he dances behind his kit,
in a trance to the beat of his drum,
in a groove, a space in his own mind.
A capsule, a membrane, solitude.
At peace when the music flows.
His whole body moving.
His precision is perfect.
Filling the room with his sound.
Dressed in black and shadow.
You can't see the light,
but the music he makes reverberates.
It's a lasting memory, you will never forget.

Dark Sister - Shadow Dance

Dark sister,
my Mad Queen.
I've seen my soul in your eyes.

Uncontrollable
Intolerable
Understandable

Dark sister,
my Mad Queen.
All the things you have seen.

Undeniable
Indestructible
Unstoppable

Dark sister,
my Mad Queen.
A broken mirror,
like shards of dragon glass.

We've all loved and we have lost.
But these actions have costs.
What world will be left?
Your soul is bereft.
The Long Night is frivolous.
Your villainous is ambivalent.
You haven't lost your humanity.
Vanity gets us nowhere.
We haven't lost.

(Continued on next page)

Dark sister,

my Mad Queen.

How long will this last?

Holes are showing in your mask.

Dark sister,

my Mad Queen.

My twin looking for a win.

I know that shadow's grin.

Trapped in your cocoon,

I hope to see you soon.

I swoon at the thought of your Grace,

a ballet so beautiful I can't keep pace.

Dark sister,

my Mad Queen.

All the terrible things you've seen.

Undesirable

Indefensible

Unforgivable

I see myself in your eyes.

Don't repeat my sins.

Your heart is deep as an ocean;

unbearable emotions.

A broken heart,

dissected by dragon glass.

A ship with holes in the mast.

This ship has sank before.

You can swim, you can swim. Swim back to me.

Dark Sister - Fire Dance

My sister,
my Sad Queen.
I'm glad to look in your eyes.

Unbearable
Indescribable
Unforgettable

My sister,
my Sad Queen.
All the tragedy we have seen.

Unbreakable
Ineluctable
Unforgivable

My sister,
my Sad Queen.
A crumbling castle,
burned by dragon flame.

We've all loved and we have lost,
but these actions had costs.
What world is left?
Our souls are compressed.
The Night was accomplished.
Astonished at our loves immunity.
All our lives there was scrutiny.
Vanity got us here.
We have lost.

(Continued on next page)

My sister,
my Sad Queen.
This ship is sailing at last.
You can take off your mask.

My sister,
my Sad Queen.
My twin, we all sin;
I know that guilt, my kin.

Trapped in this Tomb,
in your arms I bloom.
I groan for our last embrace,
a dance of tears streams down your face.

My sister,
my Sad Queen.
The cataclysm we've seen.

Unjustifiable
Irreparable
Unspeakable

Look deep in my eyes,
don't repel my gaze.
Our hearts are finally one;
untenable emotions.

A broken heart,
healed by dragon glass.
You can take off your mask.
This ship is sailing again.

We don't have to swim.
I sailed back to you.

Empty

Yes, I remember you.
How can I forget?
You were my world.
I watched you turn cold,
buried beneath the snow.
This blizzard left you frostbitten,
breathless and dying.
When you woke, from a frozen grave,
changed and unrecognizable,
I saw the blood on my hands.
My blade was sharp words,
cutting deep and stabbing true,
dissecting your heart,
leaving a scar that will never heal.
Yes, I remember you;
someone who loves me.
They are few.
I couldn't handle the beauty you brought to my life,
the passion and acceptance.
You are everything I could ever want,
but everything I knew I didn't deserve.
To me, you were a dream.
In the end, for us, it turned into a memory,
a nightmare we will never fully awake from.
Yes, I remember you.

SEVEN DEADLY

SINS

Pride

I am your god.
No matter what I do to you,
you smile and nod.
I control you.
I own you.
I can knock you down,
then pick you up and caress your cheek.
I can scream the lyrics to the saddest song,
make you cry,
then sing you a lullaby.
I rip you apart,
heart, soul, even take your body,
destroy your mind.
You are mine.
This ego,
this pride in your eyes
turned me from your Heaven
into the devil,
and I revel at the thought.

Greed

I want to be your every thought.

When I'm gone, I want you to be distraught.

I want you to feel my absence.

I want you to yearn for my return.

I want you to seek me out.

I want you to drown in sorrow and doubt.

I want to hear your heart break.

I want you to beg for an escape when I leave you here,

tied and bound,

blind in the darkness and when you can't hear a sound.

I want to make you sin.

I want to live under your skin.

I want your body, soul, and mind.

I'm the devil and I will own you in time.

Wrath

I am wrath, rage incarnate.

My soul turns black and tarnished.

I feel the flames build in my veins.

The demon woke, I'm going insane.

These once soft eyes turn to rage.

Hate has been boiling inside this cage.

You push and shove, cause so much pain.

Again and again, it's more of the same.

My hand grips your throat as you swallow.

Fire burns in my eyes, I'm empty and hollow.

You feel fear crawling up your spine.

You know you are running out of time.

You hear death knock on the door.

You feel the pounding in your core.

You turned the page, but I set it ablaze.

For I am wrath, and you can't be saved.

Envy**

Why do you have it,
and I don't?

We all want it,
secretly crave it.
That breath to fill my lungs,
that kiss to make me gasp.

Why can you touch it,
but I can't?

We all need it;
this taste of Heaven,
this burst of pleasure that fills me up.

Why should you get it,
and I shouldn't?

We all deserve it;
to feel this love,
to fill that hunger
and make me whole.

I want it.
I need it.
I deserve it.
I will have it.
It's mine.

Why can you, and I can't?

(**by Living My Rhapsody, included with permission)

Lust

All alone with this devil,
in our debauchery I revel.
Paramour you bend my ear,
whisper all the sweet words I hear.
Leaving me wanting, needing your lies.
Your whispers drain me, leave me to die.
This dream seems so real.
I know, I'm just another meal.
I feel your warm touch, the pleasure is almost too much.
You're a fiend, with a thirst that can't be quenched.
Possessed, I tilt my neck for your teeth to clench.
You suck me dry, tempt me with those thighs.
Your ample breasts are a test I always fail.
I inhale your scent.
I keep going after I'm spent.
You savor every drop and still need more.
You are my succubus, my sweet paramour.

Gluttony

As that needle tears a hole,

the euphoria leaves my life out of control.

Shedding flakes of responsibility.

Losing myself to its soul-trapping ability.

Leaving me blind to any love I once saw.

Chewing me up in its deadly maw.

Gripping whatever is left with its claw.

Squeezing my soul for every drop that is left,

I will never be the same once I've bled to death.

I've fallen into this void.

It's hard to digest.

I will never again be at my best.

This addiction will always be on my mind.

I left who I was, far, far behind.

Sloth

I am paralyzed.

I am traumatized.

Every waking moment my energy is depleted.

Even when I do nothing my energy is exceeded.

This depression is a vampire,

it leaves me fatigued and tired.

This creature sucked out every emotion,

always left thirsty for her potion.

There is no antidote for this melancholy.

This volley of never ending sorrow.

I can't function when I miss her.

Every day in between is a blur.

This sadness slumps my shoulders,

weighing as heavy as boulders.

Just slithering along.

Without you everything feels wrong.

I'm sluggish, lazy, and crazy.

This vampire consumes me, leaving me hazy.

Draining all of my joy, she is so ravenous,

stealing all of my happiness.

She leaves me crawling,

lonely, crying, and calling.

You are a flame and I am a moth.

You leave me drained and sloth.

DESTINY

Gravity (Sun Dance)

The connection was instantaneous.

Your gravity is pulling me toward your center.

Heart's heavy and life seemed to be fading.

The electricity and waves we feel when we are near

bring us back to life, igniting a fire.

A desire that is so strong everything else is meaningless.

These Twin Suns are burning with a ferocity

that would destroy most life.

But we survive and grow stronger in each other's grasp.

The fervency is so strong it lifts us up, and I feel weightless.

Even under the heaviness that has persisted before meeting you,

this dual flame burns as one,

stronger than any sun

and brighter than a candle in the darkest of night.

I love you for everything that you are.

I wouldn't change a thing.

This meeting was written in the stars.

Past

I feel like I have been separated from you at some point in the past, and now I am gravitating towards you, longing to be reunited with you. I feel like we are lost lovers from another life or another world. I feel like I know you.

When I first saw you, I missed you. It was this very odd feeling, like you were someone I was searching for. Maybe that's why I feel physical pain when I miss you, because my soul is literally torn in half, and the only way to mend it is to get back to your arms.

I have to hold back my emotions as I wait to be reunited with you because I feel like my heart is being ripped apart by my pain. The pain is physical, unyielding.

But the thought of knowing that we have found each other makes this pain bearable as I wait for you to hold me in your arms again... for the first time.

I have this overwhelming feeling that I can't lose you again. Maybe that's why I hungered for you and have, and had, this urgency to see you and to be in your arms. I don't want to miss you, in time nor in space. I feel this gravitational pull towards you.

It is becoming more powerful as time passes.

I think as we get to know each other again, it is getting stronger and more familiar. We are on a collision course that has been in the making for many years. We are destined to collide into one.

It's a dance.

We spin around and around, getting closer with each revolution.

The explosive force and the surreal calmness that will result in us coming together makes me hold my breath.

We will be there for one another as we experience the culmination of our journey to find each other... and as our new journey will begin again.

Janus

Blossom and flow

Two sides, Janus

These twin flames

Romulus, Remus

Fighting together

Legion we built

One mind, one soul, two bodies

Yet, whole

We conquer but this battle isn't won

Yet, done

We live, we thrive

We fight, and we die

Two faces, two sides

Janus, two faces, four eyes

This life lived twice

Resurrected a third time

I hope this history doesn't rhyme

One mind, one soul, two bodies, we can make whole.

Compromise

Compromise

These changes undenied

Despondent

Perplexity

This random affectivity

Unleashed

Effusion

This uncontrolled illusion

Say what you will about faith and destiny

Choking on this rhyme breathlessly

This conjoining of entities

Through time, space, and portals entry

An unabridged narrative

My soul's partitive

Our collision is imperative

A sedative for our erratic minds

Unconventional

Precarious

Yet acceptance

Treacherous waters we tread

Parlous but not hopeless

Heaven and hell

We burned and flew together

Risen from the ashes

Spirits born anew

Connected

This distance is a trial.

Seems trivial, but the physical connection is rare.

Our hearts will always be Umbilical.

Our love feeds on each other.

It keeps us alive.

Maybe this strange relationship is by design.

We feel like we've lived this time and time again.

The torture of not reaching out and touching you.

The few memories of our laughter echoing in the same room.

The moments when we make love.

So few.

I never knew a connection like this.

And we are separated by so much space.

It's a war we fight. Some battles are won, some we fail and lose,

but together, we are stronger than we've ever known;

unbreakable, even though we are two broken persons.

Together we are whole. I need you and you need me.

If there are infinite number of dimensions,

space, time, death,

we will always find each other.

And even if we lose every battle,

I will fight this war forever.

I know you know.

Ageless

With you I feel ageless,
like the young in love.
Everything is new again.
I was lost and felt hopeless,
but we found each other in this insanity.
Your beauty is mesmerizing.
I wasn't looking for this Spring;
this Season came flooding in.
Now I'm drenched in you,
soaked to the bone.
Dancing in this rain is hypnotizing.
This calm, slow dance of understanding.
No one leading, just guiding each other,
staring and lost in each other's stars.
This connection can be felt in the blackest hole,
the deepest void.
I will never be lost again.
You are my direction.
Together I see forever,
a never-ending story.
I see a lifetime with you.
In each other's arms we are ageless.

Uninhabitable

Ice

Uninhabitable
A frozen wasteland
A wilderness, thick forest
Gray clouds
No Sun shines here

Fire

Enveloped in darkness
Any traveler's foot prints
get covered in the storm.
Pelted, stoned by hail
A frozen planet
Stars revolve around you,
you pull them in.
But when too close,
it melts you,
turning you into an ocean.
And I don't think anyone
could survive it's depths.
So you push and fade,
freezing once more.
Solid ice, yet empty,
and hollow.
Uninhabitable

I am explosive Wildfire
A volcano
Unpredictable
Temerarious
Eta Carinae
I melt everything I touch
A ring of flames
A nimbus of destruction
Reaching out
Turning everything to cinders
Leaving a downpour of ashes
I burn bright,
but diminish quickly
and then ignite again.

Pulling and pushing
A constant clash of Ice and Fire

Metempsychosis

Tell me about everything
Tell me about anything
Tell me about nothing
Time is on our side
We are immortal
Metempsychosis
Death and distance are irrelevant
Entering the flesh again
We have forever
Never focusing on time
Patience and acceptance
Metempsychosis
This historical narrative
Traveling through the multiverse
Different bodies but our souls always rhyme
Seeing you at this hour...
the encounter is always familiar
Metempsychosis
It's great to see you again
If there is one thing in life I can count on it's you
We belong together
Metempsychosis

Tempo

We are the same;

never tamed and always out there.

We love each other,

intensely.

But with all our similarities,

our love for each other is different.

Our love is a compromise.

These threaded eggshells can turn into our demise.

But we step carefully,

always tender with each other's hearts.

We always dance to the same beat,

but when the tempo slows for one,

the other heartbeat speeds up;

a rhythm not expected and hard to comprehend.

We make all these plans

but never truly know what's behind the next bend.

At anytime, one of us can descend so deep,

the other can't pull them out.

This dance is exciting, wonderful, and treacherous.

But isn't that love?

Giving yourself to someone,

and letting whatever may come, come.

You know.

Disenchantment

I see you in the distance.
Unconscious, I lost control.
You're hiding; lost your enchantment.
I'm not the one you know.
You gave me your soul,
broken pieces of your heart.
We knew from the start,
space would tear us apart.
We will never be whole,
never be the same.
We will remember our names.
We have no label.
Both are unstable.
We found sanity in each other.
I don't want to know another.
You are the one for me.
You are my Everything; all I will ever see.
Blind to the world, but You are my clarity.
You lift the darkness, keep me from being heartless.
You are all I will ever need.

Out of Sync

We fall in tune, and out of time with people over the years.
Even when they are gone,
we still have a soft melody that lingers,
songs repeating in our heads.
And when it's strong, it's an orchestra.
Sometimes the timing and tempo sync beautifully.
The harmonies are there ringing out notes in perfect pitch.
Sometimes you find a rare genre,
a sound that you've never heard before,
lyrics of a story you didn't know could be written.
We may feel out of tune,
but we will be each other's tuning fork,
adjusting ourselves to life's pitch.
We compose this continues song,
a never-ending tune.
These songs may end, but they are never forgotten.
Keep singing.

Estrella

A love with a million names.
This love is not the same.
You are the one; my Person.
You are my heart and soul;
together we are whole.
Never again will we be alone.
My heart was stone,
your heart was a glacier.
I melted your frozen heart,
you chiseled my heart free.
We are released from our prison,
trembling in each other's arms.
I see a galaxy in your eyes,
stars twinkling with desperation;
needing, wanting, waiting.
An explosion of energy
when we finally collide.
Two dying stars reborn,
burning hot and bright once more.

Us

Like the rarest of storms,
we collide once every lifetime.
This storm cloud bursts violently.
This eruption sends waves through our bodies,
shaking our very existence as we tremble.
These storm clouds spread.
I feel the torrential rain pouring down,
soaking me.
The thunder is booming.
The depressed look on peoples' faces,
as our lighting strikes in multiples,
a never ending lightshow...
It truly leaves people in wonder.

OUR LOVE

Cherish

You can fall at anytime,
with anyone,
no matter what gender,
no matter what time,
love at first sight or last sight.
Maybe, it's just a moment in time.
If you find someone and fall in love,
run with it, take it to the end.
Hopefully, it will never die.
But even if it does, you will survive.
Take the minutes you have left.
If you find it, cherish it,
take it for what it is.
Take them for who they are;
love them the way you want to be loved.

Grateful

I am so grateful.
I am rich with the love you have for me.
You are a brilliant diamond.
Your beauty is unmatched.
You are the most amazing person I know,
a bright burning flame,
a match that burst to life.
When I first saw you I knew,
I had a feeling, I needed to know you.
I felt like we have met before.
I saw that you were stuck.
You feel lost.
I'm sure the feeling is overwhelming at times,
most of the time, I assume.
You have an escape, I am here.
It may not be the paradise you see in your head,
but it's what we have.
I am so grateful to get to know this gift.
You are my love and my life.

You and Me

If I had a choice,
I would choose a tiny room.
I want us to be as close as we can be.
Just a kitchen to laugh in,
and a bed to make love in.
Just you and me.
To feel your body next to mine,
our arms wrapped around one another;
the heat of my skin, the coolness of your touch,
either way, we make fire.
For once a noise we don't mind.
With love and laughter, the steam is thick.
But we can still look deep in each other's souls.
Our love is like an open window,
you can peak right in;
like a mountain, everyone can see it.
But in this tiny room, it's just you and me.

Photograph

As I lay here naked,

I see a look in your eyes I've never seen before today.

I saw your calmness as you photographed my body with your touch.

Something in you woke up, and I saw something open.

I saw sadness, and calmness, and bittersweet joy.

I also saw pain.

An hourglass almost empty.

Time was on your mind.

I saw every second pass in your eyes, yet I saw timelessness,

like we have been here again, and again.

The end is always the same.

You were looking at me from a distance,

even though I felt your touch,

and you were so close I could smell you,

and feel your warm hands on my skin.

So we soak up every drop of love we can,

every little moment.

I saw all that through your eyes;

like staring through a window at a beautiful sunset,

but not knowing what tomorrow brings.

I saw love unmatched through time, distance, pain, sorrow, joy,

happiness, and every other emotion that can be expressed.

The way you looked at me froze time,

sealed this love in my heart.

No one will ever love me like you do.

Yes, I know.

Dark Orbs

These mysterious orbs I drown in.
Staring into these dark windows,
I see sadness, happiness, but most of all love.
I can't unlock this mystery.
I see a universe unfold.
I can't look away.
Your eyes hold so much life in them.
They tell so many stories.
I've heard most of them from your lips;
I've tasted them.
But the full story is told in those dark eyes.
The things they must have seen;
the things they will see.
It's like they know what's coming.
Those orbs see everything.
I love the way they undress me.
I am completely naked when they are watching.
Those eyes see right into me, they see all of me.
Those eyes want to tell me a secret,
but it's a labyrinth I will have to solve myself.
These are windows I don't think I will ever open.
I will spend a lifetime turning the pages.
This is a novel I will never stop reading.
I am lost in those mysterious orbs.
No one has ever looked at me the way you do.

(Continued on next page)

I looked into your eyes today.

I opened those windows.

I only got a peek,

but I saw something you never showed me.

It didn't need to be vocalized.

It didn't need a pitch, a tempo, a melody.

For the first time I saw fear.

All the other furniture was still in the room;

love, sorrow, hurt, anger.

Those dark orbs always shine a bit of light.

You hide it well, but those eyes,

as mysterious as they are,

can't hide behind the darkness all the time.

Those beautiful eyes.

You are my Sun, I am your Moon.

My gravity pulls your secrets in.

I wish I didn't have to pull and drag those emotions out.

You want me to illuminate them,

but that fear I saw, those are the shadows.

You are truth, you are honesty,

but some things you won't show me.

That's okay.

What we have is time,

and one day, those shiny, dark, mysterious eyes

will show me everything.

They won't have to hide, they won't have to know fear.

Those windows will be open to me.

Sweetheart

Hey Sweetheart...
Why'd ya leave me on the groun'?
Why ya tearin' me apart?
Alone, ya don't need me aroun'?

I'm on my knees
when you come callin'
I come crawlin' Baby.
Drain' me like a vampire.
I'll feed ya when ya need me Darlin'.

No matter if I'm okay, you will be here till the end of my days.
Always shining bright, whether it's day or night.
No matter if you are here or there,
I feel your presence everywhere.
You always guide me Home,
you are my rock, my stone.
You care way more than you should,
even when I'm misunderstood.
Cause you love me, and I love you.
You lift me up when I'm feeling blue.

Hey Baby...
Why'd ya let me drown?
Why ya not tryin' a save me?
Alone, ya silent, can't hear a soun'.

(Continued on next page)

Hey my Love...
Why'd ya let me down?
Why ya pushin' and shovin'?
Alone, ya gone, nowhere to be foun'.

I'm on my knees.
You're always callin' n I come crawlin Baby,
drain' me like a vampire.
I'll feed ya when ya need me Darlin'.

No matter where you are, I hope you know I love you my Dear.
Always shining bright, whether it's day or night.
No matter if you can't hear,
my voice is always loud and clear.
I'm always guiding you Home,
you never have to be alone.
Just follow the soun'.
Baby, I'm always aroun'.
Cause I love you, and you love me.
You are everything I need.

I want to be your desire.
I want to light your fire.
But it's been burning.
You are yearning for another.

I need ya, you're my guide.
Honey, you're meltin' through my fingers.
Not sure why this love died.
I need ya; ya touch still lingers.

[Continued on next page]

But I know that's false.

You know nothing else.

I'm just another meal;

a soul for you to steal.

No matter how much I hurt, I hope you know I'm always here.

Always shining bright, whether it's day or night.

No matter if you can't see,

you can always count on me.

My heart is your Home;

you will never be alone.

I'm here for whatever you need.

With me you will always be free.

Cause I love you, and you love me.

You are everything I need.

You are different; the temperature dropped.

Your heart seems to have stopped, you're frozen and cold.

This is what's left, and I already sold my soul.

You own my heart.

Baby, you did from the start.

Roads

Complications.
So many roads,
each one takes a toll.
Each road takes me somewhere;
I might not want to be there,
but here I am.

Decisions.
So many roads,
each one takes a toll.
Each road has consequences;
I might not want to be here,
but these roads mold me. They make me who I am.

It hasn't been easy,
as on a long trip there are always up's and down's.
One stop might bring happiness,
the next a tragedy so painful,
it changes you.

Sometimes you just travel,
not paying attention.
And on those trips,
sometimes you find something you couldn't imagine;
something so beautiful, it changes you forever.

Enjoy the ride people.
You only get one.

Small Words

Love is a small word,
it doesn't seem like enough.
I don't seem like enough.
Yes Baby, I know you love me.
I know you deserve the best life has to offer.
All I can promise you is that I will try.
Every day I think of what I can do to show you,
to give you what you need.
I can't promise I won't hurt you,
I can't promise I won't make mistakes.
But what I can promise is that I will always be here
for anything you need.
Just ask and I will deliver; the best I can.
You are a very unique person.
You are my Person and I hope I'm yours.
I will swear by this till I die.
The first time I saw you,
I knew I would never forget that moment.
I didn't know anything about you,
and you swept me off my feet.
I'm not the best father.
I'm not the best person.
But I promise you I am trying.
You bring out the best in me.
Thank you for being you.

Numbing Pain

It's raining again, but this storm is different.
You feel the weather change even though we are miles apart.
You numb yourself and block your heart.
You know the pain I feel without us even speaking.
This powerful intuition is just one thing that binds our souls.
You start to feel this aching inside.
You know I'm in pain.
This roller coaster of equivocal sentiment is transcendent.
We just know.
I felt so much love from you,
but when I finally looked into your eyes I died.
This inordinate amount of sadness and happiness filled me.
Knowing I couldn't reach out and physically touch you
drained me of tears.
These aren't just tears of sadness, but happiness,
knowing that we have finally found each other.
This chaotic hurricane of emotions tears us apart,
but we will always be one, and find one another again.
This love, this pain, and the happiness.
Thank you, my Love.

Sustain

My passion is sustain,
a long ringing reverb.
My love is distortion,
a growl of potency,
echoing in one's soul;
a long note that never fades,
a melody you can't forget,
a song repeating in your mind,
a timing that is obscure...
Odd timing, hard to hear,
but fascinating to listen to.
Inducing, with a lasting effect,
this song has layers,
the volume gets loud,
but you know this song is beautiful,
and I will sing it forever,
whether you are around to hear it... or not.

Flawed

You see all my flaws.
I opened these wounds.
I bled them onto you.
You accept me, for the person I am,
even on the worst day.
When I see your face,
no matter how far away,
everything else disappears.
It's just you and me.
You are the only thing I can see.
You are so beautiful, majestic.
You are magic.
We are two flawed people,
but all I see in you is perfection.
Even in the most vivid lucid dream,
it's hard to imagine you are real.
I hope I never wake up.
I can't wait to come Home.

Swimming

We've been swimming for so long.
We are both tired, an epiphany is realized.
That Island is our place where we feel safe,
our Home.
I see you swimming.
Let's swim together.
The water is nice.
The weather on most days is clear.
That Island isn't going anywhere.
I didn't leave you,
I left the labels behind,
the rocks that weighed us down.
This way we won't drown,
only sink in each other's arms
when we swim to that Island.

Labels

Labels.

Meaningless words.

Boyfriend, girlfriend, lover.

What do they mean?

They taste good; sweet candy to the ears.

But what are they really?

Can I love you?

Can I be yours without a name?

Does it change the meaning of us?

Do we have to change the language we speak?

The words of affection we use?

Does it make us less?

The definition is the same.

The feelings and emotions.

No matter what word is used.

So, I would rather not use any.

Just the expressions of how I feel for you,

whether a touch, a call, a kiss, a hug.

Words of our affection expressed however we want.

But... I will say, I love you.

Thorns

Love is beautiful,
but it hurts.
It's like a rose;
grab it the wrong way,
and it will make you bleed.
Staring at the rose,
it's beauty,
you always want to reach out,
touch it, even when it cuts you.
Like love,
a rose without thorns isn't a rose.
True love, passion, wild love...
with no thorns, the stem would break.
Love without blood isn't true love.
If you say love doesn't hurt,
you have never truly loved.

MY LOVE FOR YOU

Cup of Tea

This is me.
Not your regular cup of tea.
I let you in the shadows.
Always guessing where the wind blows.
Our experiences aren't so different;
let's just flow with the current.
This river is spontaneous;
let's see where it takes us.
Together we can stay clear of danger,
hold each other up like marble pillars.
I can be your rock and you can be mine.
But in the meantime,
let's just have fun.

Gift

I don't have anything to offer you but myself.

I hope you like it.

I've never been more honest with anyone else than I am with you.

I keep trying to gift you with my love.

I keep finding parts of myself to show you.

Here, take my heart... it's yours.

I feel like it wouldn't beat without you.

I trust you.

Take care of it.

I won't miss it.

It's in good hands.

Without you, it's just an empty vessel.

I give myself to you completely.

The best gift I've ever received in life is you.

Execute

I show you my demons;
I have many.
You're always there to listen,
to reach out and hold me.
I am here.
Tell me your secrets.
The skeletons are filling the closet.
I am not your Judge,
the Jury, nor the Executioner.
I am here, no matter what whispers I hear.
The glass is more than overflowing;
let me take a sip, share the straw.
I am here; you have nothing to hide,
not from me; nothing to fear.
We are stronger than that.
Together these sticks will not bend;
they will not break.
I am here.

Unimagined

I can't breathe.
So many emotions.
Thinking of you.
It hurts.
I feel pleasure.
I need you close.
You are everything.
Life's riddle.
Unlocking things unimaginable.
With you, I lose myself.
Inhibition fades.
I want to show you love.
Show you affection I didn't know I could give.
Love is not big enough a word
when I think of you.

Rearview Mirror

I've never loved like this, and yes, you know.

I keep writing these words.

It's a well that is never empty.

Some of these words are love, sadness, joy, anger, regret, admiration,

fear, surprise, distraction, apprehension, ecstasy, anticipation.

This is a journey, a road we keep traveling together;

rearview mirrors we share.

I have never expressed my feelings the way I do for you;

it's hard not to.

Not that I would ever want to stop.

You deserve more love than I can conjure.

None of these endless words could ever capture how I feel.

You amaze me.

You inspire me.

I hope you are always thirsty for my love.

I hope this Lily in the Valley keeps growing.

I hope this Spring never ends.

Shattered Glass

I know I love you by the pain I feel.

My heart is a shattered glass;

all the pieces belong to you.

It's a puzzle only your touch can solve.

Your hands tracing across my skin move those pieces in place.

I know your heart feels empty and sinking, like mine.

I feel like we are being pulled together.

Yet, this barrier is between us,

this crushing feeling, this pressure.

So much stress on our hearts.

This separation feels like an infinity;

a gap that will never close.

Even at this distance, I taste the salt from your tears.

I feel your fears when we aren't near.

I can feel all of you,

all the pain, the sadness.

This missing is madness.

I need to wrap you up in these arms and hold you forever.

But this barrier keeps moving us apart.

This broken glass is my shattered heart.

Shattered Heart

I know, you feel the range.

I feel the same.

I feel the world change.

When we were apart it felt simple,

easy at the start.

But after that smile, that look,

it took everything in us to say goodbye.

It did light a fire, a drive.

I need us to survive, because if we died,

I would be lost and helpless, hopeless.

I know I love you by the gain I feel.

You make life worth living.

Our love can heal our shattered hearts.

Missing your touch across my skin ceases my heart's beat.

I know the days in between are many,

but we have plenty of time.

Let me love you.

Let me need you.

Let me want you.

This is my shattered heart.

Fix My Heart

You are a vision.

All these decisions.

My star revolves around you.

You are everything.

There isn't a second that goes by that you aren't in my head.

You are always on my mind.

I've written a million words to explain this love.

These steady thoughts and constant recollections.

These collections of memories we are starting to create.

This unexplainable connection

bringing us back to life.

The time seems to stand still.

This barrier keeping us apart.

This shattered heart...

maybe you can rebuild it.

I never thought I would have that faith in anyone.

Can you fix my shattered heart? Do you want to?

I think this is too much for you.

But I've always thought that.

I hope I'm wrong, you know.

This is my shattered heart.

I'll Try

I heard your heart break.

I won't make that mistake.

Scars need time to mend.

Sometimes just go with the scend.

Just don't let it pull you down.

I don't want to see you drown.

I don't need anything more.

I know, I'm not the cure.

In My Arms

My arms are long.
My hold is strong.
I'll never let you down.
I'm in for this 'forever ride.'
Won't shy or hide away,
I'm here to stay.
I know your baggage may be heavy.
Let me help you carry it.
Sending you all my love.
Your mind might get cloudy,
at times.
When you are ready, I'm a steady rock;
you can always lean on me.
I'll hold you up.
I wish I could take all that pain,
keep it for myself.
I would die for you,
sending you all my heart.

Inspiration

I sang a song today.
I didn't know the words.
Thinking of you, a voice came through.
All the radiance of your beauty
passed right through me.
A deliverance of inspiration.
My heart seems to revolve around you.
Your gravity pulls me in.
You shine brighter than any star,
more enticing than any sunset,
more captivating than any parable.
I want time to be motionless.
Missing you is unbearable.
In other words, I love you.

Badlands

I'm into the bad land.

I'm here to fight, to make a stand.

I hope you walk this road with me.

Through the rain, the snow,

the dark nights,

I'm here for you.

I won't leave you in the darkness.

I want you to sail with me.

This sea can be treacherous,

but together, we can accomplish anything,

conquer the world.

War is dangerous,

but together we can survive,

thrive and win.

Together forever.

Spell

I've cheated a thousand deaths,
but no battle has ever stolen my breath
as your eyes have...the beauty they hold.
You stole my heart,
control my soul.
I would swallow a million swords,
just to hear your heart's chord.
The chime is so intense;
my body trembling from the suspense.
Your touch, your kiss, your smell;
the enchantment of your spell.
I hope it is never broken.
Love should never go unspoken.

Abyss

My love is an abyss,
a deep submarine canyon,
a dangerous companion.
I can sink, or float in bliss.

My love is a sharp blade,
damaging and bloodthirsty,
belly deep, or beg for mercy.
Stay, or back in to the shade.

My love is a simple touch,
fingers dripping across your skin,
tracing, as I penetrate within.
A tender moment can be too much.

My love is complicated,
pouring out, overflowing.
My love for you is always growing.
My love is never satiated.

Relentless

I see the pain in your eyes.
I see the mask and disguise.
But Baby, you don't have to pretend;
I'm here till the end.
I won't leave, I won't stray.
I'm here to stay, Baby.
My love for you is unconditional.
My love is the rarest of kinds.
I find that I think of you all the time.
My mind is restless.
My love is relentless.
This song has repeated in my mind.
These lyrics written.
This melody I'm pickin'.
Singing this siren.
Tryin' all day and night long.
This love is so strong.
My thoughts are never hollow.
To the darkest places and fiery hell I will follow.
I wish I could swallow all your pain.
I would scrub that stain from your mind,
put you at peace even if it meant my demise.
When I look in your eyes I get this high;
I hope this love soars, I hope it flies.

Fissures

I scratch away at this Granite wall,
cracked nails, chipping, bleeding,
staining these fissures red.
I dig deep.
I stay true, as honest as I can be.
I really hope you feel me.
My words of truth aren't just for myself.
The ringing in your ears won't block me out forever.
My love is constant.
You would have to crumble a mountain
to make this love fracture.
Love, it's not a big enough a word, is it?
The scars are fissures in our minds,
deep cracks that we try to fill.
It might be easier to block them.
But they are still present.
The mountain that is building has roots
digging deep into the planet's surface.
As chaotic as things are, we stabilize this world.
This universe is vast, but here we are.
As much as you want to run,
this gravity will always pull us together.
I'm always a whisper away.
You chip away at this Granite mask.
It's hard and challenging,
but your words and questions make things tumble.
The rumble we hear is loud.
I can't hide anymore. You have opened me.
Your dissection is accurate. This fabric is thin.
You keep sowing in new layers.
It helps. Thank you.

Forecast

There are many things in my past
that make me fear things won't last.
My heart feels fragile like it's made of glass.
In the past, you have been treated crass.
You think things are moving way too fast,
but my love for you Darlin' is vast.
I wish I could predict this forecast,
I don't want the time to pass.
The wind pushing this sailing vessel's mast.
Our hearts are one and growing in mass.

Foreign

My mind is a strange land; it's so foreign to me.

Every hour, my mind focuses on a single thought.

I sink deep into that thought;

so entranced by it, it drains me.

After I'm drained, my mind races again.

I don't want to depend on anyone,

but I am starting to depend on the place I love, which is you.

It's scary.

It frightens me to know I need someone so much.

It didn't start out that way.

I didn't want that for you nor me.

You have shown me love I never thought existed.

You're a very special person; I love you for it.

You're my Person.

I found you for a reason.

You will always be my Seasons.

I will always try my best to show it.

I know I fail sometimes.

I fail you.

That makes me sink lower.

You are everything to me.

Traveler

I've traveled, far and distant,
been to many lands,
learned many lessons.
One thing that history has taught me
is that love remains a mystery.
Each love is different,
sings a new tune.
Not one of us are immune.
This cupid's harpoon is sharp,
deadly, long lasting, unfriendly.
But when that white whale,
the unlikeliest of catch,
the biggest fight,
that is worth being fought,
is caught... hold on, be patient.
Storms brew, then the sun shines through.
I know this fish in mine.
In this vast ocean,
the deepest sea,
somehow, someway, I found the one for me.

Deep Roller

This love soars and dives to its death,
to be brought to life once more,
to take a breath.
This image, doppelganger, possessor,
is omnipotent,
all powerful and controlling.
Swelling inside me to the point of burst,
my feelings cannot be contained in this single vessel.
They flow freely, spilling and pouring out upon pages.
Endless words, dripping ink and staining,
untamed love, falling fast.
I'm reaching for branches, but my grip is weak and won't last.
This attraction will be the end of me or a new birth.
But she is worth it all.
I will savor every tear drop,
the happy and the melancholy.

HOME

Alone

You want me to come Home.
You're surrounded but feel alone.
We talk all the time,
but this distance isn't kind.
It leaves us feeling heartbroken,
suffocating, like we're choking;
unable to take a breath,
leaving us wanting and bereft.
I feel the need to close the gap
knowing how much you feel trapped.
It brings me so low.
I try to be patient and take it slow.
Living in a virtual universe,
this road is hard to traverse.
But you are here by my side,
holding my hand, being my guide.

Ashore

This Island we travel...

it's ours and our love unravels.

We can be free, we can be us.

We ride this long wave.

Sometimes it crashes hard,

takes us under, but we always find the surface,

and that shoreline is always in the distance.

But we know, we will curl up and reach the shore,

wash onto the sand, together.

And here we are.

This place is our Home.

It's far from everywhere else.

Nothing can touch us in this place.

Our minds are at ease.

Our hearts are at peace.

We know the wave will swoop in,

take us away.

But we will always wash ashore again.

Together.

Homeless

Homeless, cold, and starving,
I grew used to no shelter.
Not having a bed to lie in.
Not having a blanket to hug me.
Not having a place to care for.
I let the weeds grow.
Entangling me, being devoured.
Decaying, letting life pass me by,
leaving myself to die.
Then there you are.
You saw something in this place;
a castle in the rubble, a broken palace;
a place you wanted to call Home.
We poured the foundation,
leveled out the concrete,
built a solid frame.
I can see it, this Home we're constructing.
It's taking some time, but it will last the rest of our lives.
Laid the pipes and plumbing so our conversations can flow,
so we can flush out the pain and hurt.
Our love is the insulation that will keep us warm.
Laying one brick at a time, and each one keeps us strong.
They will keep out the harsh weathers that will come our way.
And these windows let us view the beauty we are creating.
When the paint chips or the color fades,
we can always add a new coat, switch things up;
a new pallet as this Home ages.
This Home, this future, means everything to me.
We can build this together and I can't wait to come Home.

Every Time

I smell the salt from the sea.

I hear the waves crash around me.

I hear the whisper of your voice,

like the echo in a seashell.

This environment is built in my mind every time I close my eyes.

You have built a Home there.

Being with you, feeling your fingers running through my hair...

This environment is built in my heart every time I close my eyes.

You are all I see, all I feel, all I need.

Planting this seed together and watching it grow.

Turning into a field of beauty, laying in this bouquet,

watching the sun set.

This environment is built in my soul every time I close my eyes.

Watching the clouds move across the blue sky.

Like time, waiting, soon.

You are all I see, every time I close my eyes.

.

Sanctuary

How pure and beautiful is this Sanctuary.
Rays of sun and warmth resurrect me.
Blue skies and brilliant sunlight are all I see
when I am here in this Sanctuary.

When I am here in this Sanctuary,
the music is loud and her voice carries.
A beautiful poem and a steady melody,
sang only to me in this Sanctuary.

When I have to leave this Sanctuary,
my heart blackens and my mind's a cemetery.
I know this place is only temporary,
but I will be back soon in my Sanctuary.

Memories

A small world we've built.

It's getting smaller.

This is a small room.

I love this place.

Just you, just me.

Your eyes, body, mind.

Memories of you

written with my fingertips.

Five senses.

A taste, a touch, your scent, your voice,

the sight of you.

Perfection.

I wish this room had a lock

and no key.

It's the only place I feel safe in.

Free.

Just you, just me.

Wooden Box

I have a key to a wooden box.
This box is special to me.
In it, I have all I need.
The key is fragile.
I can't unlock it all the time.
When I open this box,
my sadness vanishes,
my worries float away;
I can smile again.
It breathes life into me.
I can't keep it open all the time.
When the lid closes,
I lose half of myself.
I put it back on the shelf,
I put the key in a tiny bottle...
and wait.

Marble

This marble wall is as smooth as glass,
almost perfect.
There is this one brick;
it is different from the rest.
Barely visible, but I see it with a touch.
My hand gliding across it... it moves.
A passage opens to a secret room.
There you are, my treasure, my silver,
everything I ever wanted, everything I need.
You are my secret, my special place,
my Home, a place where I am never alone.
The warmth of an eternal fire.
This secret room will always be lit.
Full and rich with my treasure,
I need nothing else, just this room.
My secret passage leading me to my place.
I've never wanted to be trapped,
but I would stay here forever if I could.
I wish... I wish... I wish.

Fantasy

You are every dream come true,
a fantasy I could never have imagined,
a beautiful Home I never thought could be built.
In your arms, I feel warm and safe.
I feel more than okay.
I never want to leave this place.
I want to stay here forever.
My heart burns when I can't hear your voice.
My mind goes cold and numb when I can't feel your touch.
Sometimes it feels like a cruel game
not being able to have it all with you.
But I will take what I can get.
I will savor every second of every moment.
It's a taste that will never become bitter.
The sweetest of flavors.
I can dine on this fine wine till the end of time.
The perfect pairing.

Diffused

Hair lightly kissed with flames,
only seen in diffused light.
Just like your emotions,
some diffused, some shine in your eyes.
The bottomless depth in your eyes,
you try to hide, but it comes through;
a little at a time, peeking,
always a gap in the curtain.
As my love grows and changes,
that gap turns into a void light.
Your mind is a traveler,
always on the move;
a vagabond, of sorts,
never resting.
You'll always have a Home.
That Home is in my heart.

Coming Home

I am running out of time.
So many things are on my mind.
I don't know why I'm so reckless.
Restless, I need to come Home.
I am tired of being alone.
I'm used to solitude,
but I have to get away.
I know she is getting worn down,
tired of drowning in my sorrows.
I can tell by the distance she's pushing away.
I can tell by the silence,
her beautiful song has gone quiet;
I can't hear her anymore.
I am coming Home.
I don't expect to feel her cool skin.
I don't expect to look into her eyes.
But I am coming Home.

Hey, Hello My Spring

Hey, hello my Spring.

Winter has come, but the birds still sing.

The flowers still bloom, and the grass is green.

It's a beautiful image, a serene scene.

Some days, rain will fall,

the snow will come down and cover it all.

But I will be here, always around.

You have been seeking a Home and now it is found.

My love is warm and as bright as fire;

you are my life, my every desire.

Even though outside looks so bleak,

my Spring is here and I don't have to seek.

I don't have to wait for my Season,

you are with me all year, you are my reason.

Burden

I've always had trouble excepting good things in my life.
For whatever reason I don't feel like I deserve them.
I've always felt that way.
I have a lot of people in my life who love me and try to help.
I hate asking for help;
I always feel like I'm a burden
and that I need to do things on my own.
I have something new in my life; I found Heaven.
This Eden is the most beautiful place I've ever been to;
I want to stay there forever.
I hate to say this,
but it's the only place I ever been where all my sadness goes away,
until I have to leave.
I also feel this garden has enough debris already and doesn't need,
nor deserves, any more.
Even though this place wants me to stay and seems okay,
it is still hard for me to accept it, but I am trying.
I wonder how much pressure this Beauty feels
with this hurricane that has landed.
I really try not to think this way, but I can't help myself.
I know this place is my Home, and I know I belong here.
I hope I am not too much pollution.
I really hope this place is okay with me living here.

HOPE

Floating

I want to take you for a ride.

Riding a tide of discovery,

you help me find myself.

I've searched this ocean,

but I keep drowning.

An endless blue and grey.

I feel your hand on my shoulder;

that touch is always there.

Some scars are barely visible now.

I used to hide and just glide through these dark waters,

floating and drifting.

You help me swim.

Things still come crashing down,

but you dive with me, not scared to swim to the bottom.

And with your help we swim back to the surface.

With your arms wrapped around me, I know I won't drown.

It may seem so far away,

but I can see the shore now.

Fountain

I have faith in this fountain.
I know I can visit anytime.
This fountain will never run dry;
a continuous, even flow.
Sometimes I like to just sit
and listen to the waterfall;
it's a peaceful sound.
I also like to cup my hands,
let the water fill up
and flow through my fingers;
lift my hands to touch my lips,
let these cool droplets trickle
as I consume them.
This revitalizing remedy is all I need;
it cures me.
This healing potion is magic.
When I'm here, I never feel alone.
This fountain will always cleanse me,
purify my soul; always makes me okay.
I have faith in this fountain.

Our Sky

Thinking of you, where we are.

We hope our sorrows will end.

Our love is a new road untraveled.

As we step forth, we know the journey is long.

There are many worlds,

but they share the same sky.

Many hearts go unnoticed and fly by,

but our Stars crossed,

and the Universe we share is ours.

It may be vast, and the distance feels like a black hole,

leaving us separated,

but I still feel your touch, I still smell you;

I still taste your lips, and unfortunately your tears when we part.

Sometimes we walk this path alone.

But I can feel your hand grasping for mine.

I know you are there; we are guiding each other Home.

We share the same sky.

One sky.

One destiny.

Ocean

You are the Ocean, wide spread, vast.
I am a stone sinking toward the bottom,
deeply soaked in you and motionless,
not being able to ride your waves.
Even wrapped up and being pulled under,
I still want to swim in you.
Such beauty in these blue waters.
Crystal clear.
I know.
I see everything.
Even during storms and rough tides,
the erosion over time, the changes...
We survive the weather.
I am unmovable; a solid rock.
I am Granite and you are my Ocean.

Memories

Alone in this Universe
A curse lifted
Gifted with an Angel
A celestial being
Seeing things anew

Evolving, changing
Taming me, my hearts grown
Expanding, unraveling
Traveling through the unknown
No expectations

Revolving, aging
Time infinite
So many stars
Heaven, my Eden
All these pretty things
All these recollections

Chisel

You feel frozen in this fossil,
in this dark space.
Heavy gravity.
You're drifting.
A black hole.
Soulless and no control,
floating paralyzed,
mind empty,
can't analyze.
This air is thick,
suffocating,
petrified.
I'm going to break through this Granite.
This mountain of stone won't stop me.
Hammer and chisel in hand,
I won't let this love fizzle.
I will chip away at this exterior;
I will find that center in you.

But I'll Try

Seeing you cry makes my heart ache.

There is so much at stake.

I want to see what's around the bend.

I hope this River never ends.

Never want my feet to touch the ground.

Your voice is the sweetest sound.

Your heart is mine, mine is yours.

I know, I'm not the cure,

but I'll try.

Endeavor

I see hope on the horizon.
I see a new sunset; so mesmerizing.
I feel a comforting breeze.
I feel the calmness, I'm feeling at ease.
I see an old demon rise,
and see a new love die.
I know you mean the words you say,
and I really hope you stay.
I see a brightness; a new dawn.
I hope you are Home and not gone.
I know nothing lasts forever.
You are here now, for this endeavor.
That is all anyone can ask.

Tired Dreams

This was a long dream.

It seemed to go on forever.

But we finally pulled back from being entwined.

I saw the look in your eyes;

like this dream was manifesting into a nightmare.

We both know the dark times that creep around the corner,

that hide in the shadows;

they are always present;

we can't escape them, but just endure.

There is a Spring in the distance.

This Season may take longer to visit,

but we both know it will come.

Garden

My heart is fleeting, feeding,

digging through depths I don't understand.

Feeling stranded by these times of trouble.

I still see Beauty in the distance.

I still see what we have is magnificent.

These times of turmoil will fade.

Together we will move to happier days.

My Beauty brings light to my shadows,

fends off the darkness that is attached and follows me.

Even in the worst seasons, the soil is fine.

The seeds of life we plant will grow in time.

I am patient, I know my Spring will come soon.

The Garden we are planting won't grow in a day.

As hard as it is to be away from my Sanctuary,

I know, my Beauty, our love is fertile.

I can't wait for these flowers to bloom.

Moon and Star

I made a promise never to go,
but in my times that are so low,
fear sets in and my duality
shows its mask and my fallacies.

My love for you is rich as a king,
even when my words bite and sting.

You are my Moon, bright and silver;
I am your Sun shining and familiar.

When the Sun sets and then dies,
and night comes with no Moon in the sky,
even invisible, they are still there;
the Moon misses the light, Sun's in despair.

Morrow will come, Sun will rise at dawn,
and someday a full Moon will sing her song.

JOY

Emerald

I wasn't searching for this treasure,
but in this dark tomb, I found an Emerald.
It's worn, and was lost,
calling to me all this time.
A humming, a vision in my dreams.
Your chants were songs,
calling me, making wishes;
summoning me to your side.
Here I am, amazed and in awe.
This jewel is priceless to me.
I want to keep it forever,
store it in my heart
with all my other treasures.
None of the others give me this kind of pleasure.
Not much for riches and gold,
but you are my heart and soul.

Blow Me a Kiss

Blow me a kiss
from where you are.
Your love will reach me soon.
Send me your best wishes,
hugs and kisses.
It's a big world.
Our love is immeasurable,
pleasurable, yet vulnerable.
A broken heart that keeps repairing.
It's whole when you are near;
destroyed, pierced, and speared
when you are gone.
Alone without my heart and soul,
you are the only thing that makes me whole.
I need that kiss, to be lost in our abyss,
where the world vanishes,
along with all our sadness.

Unspoken

As you touch these lips,

the look in your eyes makes me smile.

You love the feel.

You love the taste.

You love the sweet words that are spoken.

You can't get enough of them.

All of the 'I love you's that come out

are never too much.

I love the look on your face when you trace my lips.

It's an unspoken 'I love you,'

one that I feel deeply.

I never understood why,

but it always makes me feel at Home.

You know.

Swimming

We swam again
to our tiny Island.
A bed of roses.

Such beauty,
covered in your pedals.
Soft, warm touch.

My Spring is here.
It won't last long enough,
but I will enjoy the weather.

Soak in the Sun.
The clear blue waters.
Not worry about tomorrow.

Living the moment.
Dusk will come soon,
but so will the dawn.

Clear Skies

More beautiful than the sun setting.
Sitting, staring till the sun rises;
fretting at the time, sweating.
Still your voice.
Your mind surprises.
You always read my heart,
know exactly what to say.
I couldn't fathom us to depart;
a second away makes the world grey.
But I know the sky will clear;
these clouds will part.
There's always tomorrow my Dear;
a new painting, a song, lyrics of our love;
the finest art.

Ether

I see you.
Honest and true,
a bright light.
You clear this fog,
bring me sight.
A feeling I rejected;
a feeling that was oblivious,
lascivious, yet serious.
Affected by your affection.
Floating in this ether,
my feet never grounded.
This must be a dream.
It feels like Heaven.

Hey

Hey Sweetheart.

I feel like I'm floating right now.

Living on a cloud.

My love for you is so strong;

I feel like I'm about to burst.

My love is spilling through every pore.

I've never felt this way before.

I may miss you, but I feel you are here with me,

holding me, hugging me,

kissing me, loving me.

Precious

It's so nice to see you.
It's been a while.
We never get much time,
but the time that we do get
is precious to us.
It's always nice to take you in,
to watch the way you see me.
No one else sees me in that light.
Most of the time,
when people see me,
it's in darkness.

Lavender

She's twirling in fields of lavender.
Her beauty makes me bemused.
Her scent of flowered perfume
sends my body into percussive waves,
like cascading rain drumming a tune,
sends thrilling chills rippling through my skin.
My life's evolving into something new,
changing everything,
making me whole again.
I'm battling in fields of chaos,
but when she sings we're equidistant.
She's a muse, an angel, possessing me,
showing me who I want to be.
We're living in singularity.
Looking into a mirror,
and through her eyes, I see clearer.

Joy and Sadness

We swam to our Island today.

It's been so long.

The swim was tiring.

We were both so worn out.

We did enjoy ourselves,

laying in the sand,

watching the blue sky,

watching the changing colors as the sun dipped low,

feeling the Summer's heat,

lost in each other's eyes,

and breathless in the embrace.

Melody

Hearing your melody I feel so many emotions;

elation, ecstasy, enrapture.

These emotions are quite real, serious.

My heart is overflowing beyond capacity.

I don't feel consternation, or agitation, nor trepidation.

I feel assurance.

Calmness.

Happiness.

I feel loved.

I'm thankful for this overwhelming sensation.

Delirious.

Euphoric.

Knowing you, is a symphony, a dance never ending.

This dance, a ballet, a waltz, a tango...

neither of us leading, but we're one; together.

Soul, body, spirit, mind; one.

A thousand miles apart, but when I hear your song,

I can feel your touch, gentle; your glance, subtle, inviting.

I forget to breathe, but air is irrelevant when I'm with you.

I can live on your love alone.

I love you more than I can express with any composition.

Shield

I feel your love wrapped around me like a shield.
Your love has been a blessing,
so many parts of me you have healed.
I can't imagine what life would be like if you weren't here.
Even though you are not close, I always feel your presence.
I smell your incense, I feel your fingers dig into me,
carving out a place in my heart,
making me feel at Home.
I need to hear your voice when I wake up.
It reminds me I'm alive;
like hearing the birds sing when the sun rises.
You are the light that shines through my window.
You are the warmth I feel when I am alone at night.
You are more than I ever expected.
You are my sunshine, my clear skies,
the most beautiful shade of blue.
You are a dream come true.

All She Sees

All she wants is me.
The Person I am is all she sees.
She isn't expecting anything but affection.
My soft touch is all she needs.
It's freeing to know someone like you.
You don't care about my looks;
what you see is my love for you.
You look into my eyes and realize
I will always love you.
There is nothing you could do
that can change my opinion of you.

Colors

This silent film
Black and White
Dark nights
Colorless days
Drifting along, aimless
Rinse, repeat
Stagnant
Surprised
One morning, I woke up to a sky
I've never known.
A light peaking over the horizon.
Hues of blue
Deep purples
Orange and red, like fire.
It was beautiful
Since I've seen this light,
this painting of many colors,
shades of brilliance,
rays of warmth,
making me bloom once again,
I've never known happiness like this;
not till you brought color
into my world.

Robin

So many voices singing.
Each bird sings a tune;
chaotic, yet melodic.
There is one voice,
carries over the others.
A Robin.
Bright red.
Her song steals my heart,
flies to me in the morn,
sings to me at night.
Robin always perches near,
her voice I always hear;
making sure I'm okay.
Please, never fly away.

HEAT

Cosmic Matter

I feel this universe has handed me a gift.

You're a cosmic force that lifts me up, holds me so I don't fall.

I'm incredulous wondering...do I deserve this?

A sedulous pursuit to show you I love you.

Falling deep and deeper into you,

getting lost and never wanting to be found.

Inside you, I will never tumble down.

Floating on you like a wave,

craving everything you have to offer.

Melting into you...

This ecstasy is Heaven and can last an eternity.

Your touch holds the heat of a thousand suns,

tracing my existence overwhelming every breath I take.

Deeper, deeper, climaxing to euphoria,

as our breath becomes rhythmic, deeper, louder, concurrent...

I surrender; I am yours.

Heaven

When I saw you there, naked,
I saw you in a new light.
The shades and colors were brighter.
I didn't want to ravage you at the moment.
I wanted to paint you.
I've never seen anything so beautiful.
I traced you with my fingers for hours.
I know every inch of your skin,
every freckle.
I wanted that moment to last forever.
It really was Heaven.
I would die right now to be there again.
I am lost in you,
and I don't ever want to be found.

Crown of Fire

I have a red halo,
a crown of fire.
You see me as an angel,
but I know I'm the devil.
I possessed you,
lured you in with my charm and fiery touch.
My kiss melts,
my tongue burns;
I am very satisfying,
full of passion.
I am perilous.
When this nimbus of fire blazes,
spreads through me,
starts to consume,
can you quench this fire
before it incinerates you?

One

The static was drowned by traffic,
the pouring rain and thunder.
The deep gaze in your eyes.
An Island of trust.
Such a close space,
closing such a gap,
the depth of our separation.
Becoming one, the same heart.
Dancing souls, twin flames.
As we became one,
again in that moment,
space and time,
and every fear was abandoned.

Moonlight

Gasping for a breath, eyes locked, panting. This hunger, this craving is unstoppable. We smile because we know it's not over. We feed off each other's energy. Our appetites for each other are gluttonous, our thirst is unquenchable. We starve for each other like the wild. Lying down and watching me as I climb on top of this mountain. Staring in your eyes as I guide you inside. We are enchanted with passion, excitement, all restraint is gone, no distance, no holding back.

I take you, placing my hand on your chest, grabbing your shoulder. I start riding you hard and furiously. The absolute pleasure in our eyes is palpable. We are lost to the world in each other. Your moans are piercing, emphatic and demanding responses. I match your volume as I take you. Yes, Baby, yes. Your big hands grabbing me and pulling me into you. I sit up and look at you with such lust, you melt. Arching my back and moaning so loud I almost scream. A current of rapture washing over us. Euphoric and breathless. Yes, yes Baby.

As we lay there panting and breathless. You kiss me and smile seductively. I reach down and touch myself with a steady hand. I go down and tease you. My tongue dancing around your tip. My eyes are smiling at you. I take you into my mouth. You moan quickly and loudly. I feel your body vibrate as I taste you. I love watching you.

You move your hand to grab me by the back of my head. I hear you moan as I take you all the way down. You grip the sheets, and my head tighter. The look in your eyes is just as satisfying as my actions.

As I bend over, filling my mouth with your love, I reach down to rub that spot I love so much. I lift my head up, bite my lip, and smile slightly, working my hand at a steady pace on you and myself. I stop touching myself and have a taste. The moan of delight that comes out of my mouth drives you senseless. You push my head back down so I can take you in my mouth again. I start to rub my sweet spot. We feel the pressure building, our moans getting louder and faster. I pick up the pace. The explosion that follows takes us by surprise, I swallow everything and come up to kiss you. I have something better planned for later, but I needed you now.

Crescendo

This sweet music we are composing is hypnotic,
mesmerizing.
The volume is soft and rhythmic,
but building, getting stronger.
Singing in harmony,
the chorus is swelling,
vibrating our bodies, trembling;
hearts racing, drumming.
The tone is deep,
booming, deafening, climatic.
My fingers tracing across your skin.
Your arms wrapping around me,
pulling me in, holding me tight.
The tempo increases.
Everything around us disappears.
In this concert, we are one.
The release leaves us breathless,
and craving more.

Hot Stones

You miss my touch.

My hands are like warm Granite,

hot stones that make you melt;

strong vices gripping you,

but gentle when they need to be.

You miss my voice; this soothing sound that penetrates your

mind, rocks your body.

You miss my smile; that look in my eyes.

No one has ever looked at you the way I do.

When I love you, my eyes, my smile, make you shiver with

pleasure.

You still feel my embrace; nothing has made you feel so safe.

I miss your skin; like velvet, so smooth, addictive.

The way you kiss me; those lips...

My god...

Your voice in my ear; the pleasure you feel.

My fingers across your body; every inch as satisfying as the last.

Your laughter; that laugh is music.

The way you look at me, you see something no one else sees.

You see Me, and you like what you see.

I know.

Passionate Games

You love my body;

you know it so well.

Your warm, strong hands draw beads of sweat across my body.

This wave of heat hits me,

as boiling as your touch; my body shivers.

Your touch goes deeper,

as my voice carries.

The look in your eyes and the smile on your face widen.

Those lips, that look,

make me melt into you.

You start to sing as my volume increases.

You never take your eyes off me.

You write beautiful lyrics with your fingers.

These Summer games last all Season.

You love me.

You know me so well.

Solar Flare

Yes Baby... as I fill you up with my love, my moans so intense they echo like a primal scream. I know we have just begun.

I love you Baby. I kiss you long and hungrily, I want to devour you, Baby. Hearing us sing together makes me ravenous, fuels my fire for you. I wrap my knees around your hips, grabbing your legs and putting them on my large strong shoulders. I slide deep inside you, grabbing you tightly by your thighs with my thick, strong hands. Feeling you shiver as I slide in deep, taking control... losing control. My moans are thunderous. The pleasure of you possessing me. The sound of your voice, the touch of your skin, your scent, the taste of you, the look in your eyes. Everything about you overwhelms my senses. Yes, Baby, yes.

I can't help myself, as I roll your leg over and slide behind you. Holding your hips. You reach down to caress yourself. Then tease me as you lick your fingers and move your hand back down. You grip my arm with your other hand to steady yourself from the intensity of my thrusts. Long and deep rhythmic dance. We are one. Yes, yes... pulling you closer to me. This fire is burning bright and the heat builds. We can feel the build coming as we both chorus in unison, quivering uncontrollably.

Sugar

You taste so sweet.

Like sugar, you melt on my tongue.

The heat from your breath...

As you moan and sweat,

you shiver at my touch,

needing and wanting me so much.

I feel your body quiver,

I feel your fingers clutch my hair,

grasping and gasping as I stare.

I love the look on your face;

your lips part as my tongue starts;

my hands grabbing your hips.

I love the look in your eyes;

the shape of your lips when you sigh.

My hands gripping your thighs.

The pace increases as my tongue traces.

Your breath gets shorter, your muscles tight.

A smile spreads across my face at the sight.

I feel you arch your back, at the moment of climax.

I fucking love it.

Selenelion

I see us standing at the foot of a bed. There is just enough light coming through the window that we can see each other's eyes. I can't take my eyes off of you. You are so beautiful. I love you. I place my hands on your hips and move in to kiss you. The kiss is soft, gentle but you can feel the hunger radiating off my body. My heart is pounding. My arms wrap you up; I want to feel you close to me. Kissing you deeply, the hunger increases, but the touch doesn't. I lean back a bit and look into your eyes. I lift your shirt off and kiss you again. I never stop kissing you. I guide you to the bed, lay you down. I climb on the bed never taking my eyes off you. I slowly take your pants off, we smile at the slight struggle as you lift up your hips. I take your underwear off. I sit back on my knees and take you all in. God damn you are absolutely stunning. I start kissing the top of your thigh, cautiously. When I get to the point you think I want to be, you feel my breath cross over and kiss the inside of your other thigh. Then I slowly start kissing and moving up, the whole time never unlocking my gaze from your eyes. I pause as I get to your breast, take my time, kissing them, kissing your nipples, my tongue slowly dancing. Then I move up and kiss you intensely. You can feel me close to you where you want me but not going there just yet. I pull my head back just a bit, look into your eyes and say, "I love you." I watch you as I slide inside you. I tremble as I enter you, the look of pleasure on your face fuels my hunger for you but still gentle, slow paced, deep, penetrating. The sound of your moans drives me insane; I match the magnitude.

The world disappeared the moment I first saw you, and this is Heaven. My hands are everywhere, seeing with them. Your breasts, thighs, touching your cheek. The kissing is passionate as I slide deep inside. I kiss your cheek, whisper in your ear, "I love you."

Cupids' Arrows

There is no one like you.
You make this magic work.
You sacrificed yourself,
just to make sure I'm okay,
to show me how love works.
I'm so enchanted by us;
swept away by your spell.
Your smiles are cupid's arrows,
raining down on me.
Each one you fire hits Home,
and makes me fire back.
Your voice is a siren's song,
alluring, captivating.
Your eyes make me feel I'm Home.
I never believed in angels
until you spread your wings.
Your touch is nirvana.
Your legs wrapped around me,
eyes connected, lips pressed.
The melody of our breaths.
I will always have my Spring,
my beautiful Poppy.
This love will last through time.
Forever my Valentine.

LONGING

Beauty

I dreamed of such beauty.
It made me cry.
Felt undeserved, so I denied.
The dream keeps recurring,
the whispers keep whispering,
sending me love,
showers of kisses.
A dream that is dreamt,
replayed time and time;
her love for me, is so divine.
Her fingers dig deep,
reaching my core.
I can never have enough,
I always want more.
She will always be there,
staring with those eyes.
Without her, my heart shrivels,
withers, and dies.

Devil on Your Shoulders

I see an old demon standing on your shoulder.

I wonder, will it turn into an angel.

It is hard seeing the past, present, and being blind to the unknown.

I know that you are my Home.

I want all of us.

I miss you and need to be by your side.

All the windows in my past are closed.

I'm glad you are venting and healing.

I hope someday that I am your Home,

that I can be there next to you.

I'm sorry that my mind wonders sometimes.

Especially when I'm sad.

I hope you know that you are my Everything,

and that I know you love me.

This is a jumbled mess of thoughts,

but I have to get them out somehow.

I've never loved someone as much as I love you.

I didn't think it was possible or that I would even want to.

I probably should have thought about this more,

but I had to say something...

I love you so very much and miss you,

and can't wait to see you.

Deja Vu

I've never known hunger like this,
this need for sustenance.
I'm starved and thirsty.
I have the most decadent spread,
but I'm starting to lose my appetite
as I watch this meal rot,
and my energy fades.
Dying alone in a desert.
Just a mirage of memories,
a deja vu;
a reminder of past lives,
dreams of loss;
nightmares of present.
A premonition of... I don't know what.
Here we are, deprived,
desperate for a taste,
malnourished of our love.

Restless

I'm feeling impatient.

Anxiety is taking over.

I'm so restless.

There is only one remedy,

but that alchemy is miles away.

I know you feel it too.

We both need it.

The warmth of our bodies,

the feeling of being in each other's embrace.

I feel like I'm angry at an abstract thing.

But this distance, this barrier, has substance.

It is a real, physical pain.

Nothing can fill this emptiness, but you;

being next to you.

I need the other half of my heart.

It won't beat without you.

I can't breathe without you.

I need to exhale.

But I will hold this breath

till we meet again.

Desperate

I'm so lost,

hidden in this thick forest.

It's so dark, pitch black.

I hear nothing

but my own breath.

I see no stars,

no Moon.

This valley is deep.

I am too exhausted to climb out.

This depression traps me,

keeps me from being alive.

I do see a small flicker

peeking through these branches of despair.

I hope to hope.

I wish to leave this place,

but I keep getting lost.

I find myself here,

far, far away from where I want to be.

I miss you.

Journey

There is so much distance
from one Island to the next.
I hear your voice but can't see you.
It's so relaxing to know you're here.
At the same time,
this Island is so big.
I feel the separation.
I miss you, my Darling.
As I travel and time goes on,
I see your face and hear your voice.
This Island is vast,
but not the jungle we are used to.
I feel so close to you, yet still can't touch you.
As I travel and time goes by,
this Island gets smaller,
completely barren, except for you.
These moments are worth the journey,
the rough waters, the hard choices,
all the struggles since we washed ashore.
I can hear you, I can see you, I can reach out and touch you.
Your cool skin, your smell... I can taste you.
You are always near, no matter how far.
I love you, Sweetheart.

Distortion

I'm struggling so hard.

Everything is so heavy.

My mind is so distorted.

Even the simplest thing

feels like I'm learning to walk.

I keep stumbling over myself.

The worst thought, is losing you.

I feel like if this doesn't stop, you will vanish.

I've never been scared of losing you.

It's also been a long time since I had something to lose.

I don't know how these words will resonate,

I love you more today than I ever have,

I miss you and need to see you.

Unfocused

You absorb me.

Filling you up.

Overflowing, changing you.

You distort me.

Unfocused.

Overwhelming, changing me.

I feel the push.

This distance is growing.

Both over-encumbered.

This weight keeps us from connecting.

There is some barrier expanding,

keeping us apart.

The lights are dimming;

if we blink, the other may disappear.

You control me.

Torrent, erosion,

sediments, pieces of me evacuating.

This current has changed.

You need to break free,

let these rapids take you.

Let go,

or let me in.

Enhance

There is so much distance between you and me,
but I have never felt closer to anyone else.
There isn't a second that goes by that I don't think of you,
that I don't think of how I can show you the way you deserved to be
loved.
I don't think I do it justice.
But as long as you will have me, I will keep trying.
When I am missing you, I feel like I'm dying.
But then we talk, and I feel like I'm flying.
Every problem disappears;
everything that I'm happy about is enhanced.

Candle

This candle burns.
The light is bright.
The scent is overwhelming.
Sometimes, I want to blow this flame out
instead of watching it fade.
The slow burning is torture,
yet it is so beautiful.
Most of the time it's comfort, excitement,
but sometimes, it sets my heart ablaze.
The hurt, the burning inside,
the scars I know that will be left behind...
Should I blow this flame out,
or take this candle for what it is?
I can light it whenever I want,
I can let its perfume fill the room.
But I want this flame to last forever.
Right now it's casting a shadow.
And no matter what the angle, I am in the gloom.

Belle

I rode to town to see my Bell.
She rang a familiar tune,
saved me from my hell.
It was difficult to say my farewell.
I hope to see her soon.
I hope I can tell that she's doing well,
that I saved her from her hell.
Even if it's just for a while,
I love to see her smile.
She is everything to me.
I hope that's what she sees.
When I listen to her needs,
I will be there, I can set her free.
Even if it's just for a while,
I love to see her smile.
She is everything to me.
I hope that's what she sees.
When she looks at me,
I hope I'm everything she needs.
I love her, and I hope to see her soon.

Light and Dark

The Sun has set.

I seep into the darkness.

This is a cycle like any other.

There must be a midnight to the dawn,

I guess.

It seems like torture to endure all the happiness,

and to be dropped into this grave soon after.

The loneliness, the missing.

I can still feel you next to me,

but you are not here.

Waking from this heavenly dream,

just to be thrust into this insidious nightmare,

to be bathed in your warmth,

and then drenched into an ice-cold river,

drifting in this vast universe, this space...

waiting for gravity to pull us together again...

Time is all we have; and distance.

But eventually, we will drift near and be pulled together again.

In the meantime,

I am here,

wanting.

Antidote

It hurts the most not being near you,
but I know there's not much we can do.
Not hearing your voice puts a hole in my soul,
but when we talk again, you make me whole.
Some people might think this is juvenile,
but caring about others' opinions ain't my style.

I miss you so much, Baby... all the time.
Looking at your face makes me smile.
Out of touch for a long, long while.
Vicariously living through others' rhymes.
Everything seemed dark and obscure,
but under the shine of your light, I'm cured.

Look

Looking deep inside.

What did I find?

Nothingness.

Opening these drawers,

looking in this closet.

Barrenness.

Air. A breath.

Trying to feel.

Just vacant.

Only one thing fills the space, it's you.

Everything else is just more emptiness.

Saying Goodbye

Even when you are sad,
you look so beautiful.
Wanting to hold me a second longer.
You wear this disguise.
I know your heart is cracking,
pieces shattering.
Love is painful.
Those that say it isn't,
haven't experienced all of love.
We know I have to go;
I can't help but let these tears flow.
You pretend to be strong.
You whisper sweet words in my ears.
You hold my face in your hands.
You wipe the tears from my eyes.
You tell me everything's okay.
You say you need my arms around you.
I need to feel your lips one more time.
You need to feel my deep embrace.
This parting is only temporary.
But it feels like forever.

Angel

I've never believed in Angels
till I saw you spread your wings.
Like a free spirit in the snow,
so beautiful, like no one I've known.
I miss watching you dance;
as unique as the snowflakes that fall.
All I see now is the shape in the cold,
where I watched you dance.
I feel like I'm just a shadow,
dark and transparent,
not the one you fell in love with.
You miss watching the sunshine
on the pale flakes.
You're always so bright.
My golden sun has dimmed,
but the silver of the moon
still shines for me.
We seem to keep missing one another.
But sometimes, the Moon shows during the day
as the Sun rises, painting the sky
with the colorful pallet we love so much.
But this juxtaposition of Ice and Fire,
the rising of my sun,
is melting the image of you dancing.
The snow is starting to fall,
your silhouette is starting to fade.
I want to see my Angel dance again.

Chasing Shadows

I long for my Moon.

You are so far away.

I can't see you tonight.

Even when we get close,

I only illuminate portions of you.

I've never seen the full view.

I know the angle has to be just right,

the timing has to be perfect.

But there are things you don't want me to see.

You hide well. That dark side.

Even when I get a glimpse, I'm just chasing shadows.

I have never seen all of you.

I know I've shed light on some of you,

and I've seen more than most.

I find every part of you beautiful.

I love the little parts that brighten when I am near,

the ones that only I see.

The pieces of you where my light reflects are precious to me.

Grazing your surface with my fiery touch.

I know how much you crave this Star's kiss.

I know you well, but I still hunger for more.

This cycle will continue forever.

This universe is infinite.

We will always find each other,

and one night I will see you fully.

My light will shine on you,

and your love will reflect back on me.

Morning Bird

This fear shouldn't be here;
I know you won't disappear.
I hear your voice, loud, clear...
I feel your love, my Dear.
My Darling, my Sweetheart.
My Starling, it hurts to be apart.
We're off to a perfect start.
It's your love, strength that you impart.
My Dove, let me say a few more words...
you are my Robin, my high flying bird.

Taste

Hey my Person,
I'm thirsty.
I need to take a sip of you;
just a little taste.
It feels like a lifetime
since I felt your embrace.
The missing is getting worse,
and I know you feel it too.
I love you, and I miss you.

Hey my Sweetheart,
I'm hungry.
I need to take a bite;
just a little taste.
I miss your touch at night.
That smile on your face.
This missing is a curse.
But I know your love is true.
I love you, and I miss you Darlin',
and you know.

MY ANGEL

Original

No one can cover you.
A true original.
Knowing you is an adventure,
a journey I want to last forever.
I never want to say "goodbye."
When you are gone, I want to die.
My heart feels broken.
A storm of sadness,
emptiness only you can fill
with your voice and touch,
with your love.
I belong to you.
You belong to me.
I can only deal with the pain,
knowing you are here.
Even being so far apart
you are always near to my heart.

Sometimes

Sometimes you are a pill that's hard to swallow.

In your absence, I feel very hollow.

As I choke this down,

I found I'd rather have you sometimes,

than never at all.

As high as I fly, sometimes I fall,

and these lows are dark.

I know there is a sunrise somewhere.

I'm hoping to see that light pierce the clouds soon.

I miss those colors.

Right now I just see doom.

The gloom that is following me,

frightens me, and blinds me to what I know is real,

steals my happiness and robs me of myself.

It's a battle that will never be won, just sustained.

But I'm a fighter and this is worth fighting for.

It's worth the scars, the pain, the strain.

I hope you know.

Lily

Planted in a beautiful valley.

Sounds of flowing streams.

Trickling water falling.

Birds singing.

Tall trees, with vibrant red leaves.

Clouds of the purest white.

A light breeze, tickling your tepals.

Wind blowing, sending a sweet scent.

A Sun with rays of gold,

lightly warming your stem.

Thriving in a Goldilocks environment.

Things have to be just right.

But even in the night,

your brilliant bells ring silver.

The Moon reflecting the Sun,

your face reflecting the cool shine of the Moon.

Unparalleled beauty, iridescent.

Your temperature and hue change,

but your Belle stays the same.

Moth to a Flame

I know what you see is a moth,
but what I see is a butterfly.
What you see is old and abandoned.
I'm here and I see perfection.
I will never reject you.
I will always see the truth.
It's been hard for you to fly.
You see yourself in black and white,
but the colors I see are effervescent.
The scales on your wings are thicker than most,
almost dragon-like.
I know you can breathe fire if you need to.
You can also be graceful in your flight.
I know you feel like your fire is being extinguished.
Your light is dimming and might flicker out,
but you are my Polaris,
always guiding me Home.
You are also my Sirius,
the brightest star in my sky.
You may feel like someone plucked your wings,
but I still see them, and I know you can still fly.

No Matter

No matter where I gaze, you are always there.

Always shining bright, whether it's day or night.

No matter if you are near or far, you are the brightest star.

You always guide me Home. You are always in sight when I'm alone.

You care way more than you should.

You would be here tomorrow if you could.

Because you love me and I love you.

There is nothing you wouldn't do.

Hidden

I can see you in the dark.
You are beautiful in any light,
or none at all.
I see the brightness flickering,
showing who you really are.
You're so apprehensive.
I wonder why.
The person you are doesn't belong to anyone but you.
It hurts me to know the beauty is hidden behind that mask.
Everyone should see it, especially you.
I wonder what you see in the mirror.
How clear is the image?
Is it hard to look into those eyes?
Sometimes, you feel like it's okay to come outside
and play.
But other times, you're hiding;
the shade is safe and the mask is normal.
No one can find you there, not even you yourself.

Muse

You are my Muse.

You inspire me to want more from this life.

I stopped dreaming a long time ago,

but knowing you, and having you in my life,

makes me think anything is possible.

You woke me up from this deep slumber.

You bring so much joy to my life.

The way you make me feel is unexpected.

I didn't know I could feel this way.

Loving you is the greatest feeling.

Knowing you love me is indescribable.

Everything about you triggers some sensation in my body and my mind.

Your scent, your touch, my hands on your body, that look,

that beautiful laughter.

If there is a Heaven, it's in your arms.

If there is a hell, it's when we are apart.

But I will walk through the fire, the dead of Winter, any battle,

to be next to you.

I miss you.

I need you.

Most of all, I want you.

Unbreakable

Your love is so strong,
unbreakable.
Nothing can penetrate it.
Unshakable.
Your honesty sometimes gives me pause,
makes me think, makes me ponder.
You're a wonder.
Our twin flame will never sunder,
never be extinguished.
This light will shine bright,
an eternal flame,
burning deep into the night,
and still rise and set the sun.
Our hearts burst and set the world
ablaze.
Your gaze melts me.
Ya know.

Ice Cream

I wish a smile grows on your face.

You're beautiful as a daisy.

Your love drives me crazy.

I hope you have the best day.

Laughter and joy is a blessing.

I'm fortunate enough to see it often.

A kiss on the cheek makes my heart soften.

Your love is sweet like ice cream.

Having you in my life is a dream.

Together we make a great team.

Darling, you make every day perfect.

Dream

She was a dream that was dreamt, yet reality.

I felt her touch.

I smelled her scent.

I heard her voice.

I know the choices we make won't last;

but this is a forever.

The love we have is our Heaven.

I wish nothing would ever change,

but I know nothing will be the same.

Not sure who's to blame.

No one is.

The result is so simple.

A fix that doesn't have to be mended

because nothing is wrong.

Neither of us are pretending.

The words are spoken

and chosen correctly,

even if they are misunderstood... at times.

This time, this moment, is where I want to be.

Wish

You have one wish, and it's to fly.
You want to feel the air beneath you,
feel the freedom of soaring,
gliding to new skies,
seeing the world.
You have one wish, and it's to be healed,
have your broken wings mended,
to have your black feathers
show their true beauty.
The colors you know are there,
but no one sees them.
You have one wish, and it's not to cry.
You want those tears to dry,
feel the freedom of happiness,
shedding your skin to the real you,
the world seeing who you are.
You have one wish... to have your world,
to have someone to fly with you,
and not for you.
You have one wish...
to be loved the way you know you can love.

Machine

I am a Robot
that tailors itself to the individual.
Just turn the key.
I was designed just for you.
I will say the things you want to hear.
I will move the way you want me to.
I will dance.
I am a Machine.
This is the way I was built.
Almost a perfect design.
My gears freeze,
but the mechanism still turns.
I am what everyone needs but no one wants.

Inhale... Exhale...

You scream in the darkness,
begging for release.
Just a moment to breathe,
a second to take a breath.
Inhale, exhale.
You didn't expect a response.
A calling. It started as a soft vibration.
You asked a question,
made a wish,
begging for the pain to cease.
Inhale, exhale.
You have been trapped in this darkness for so long.
You didn't expect a flash.
Just a flicker; it was blinding.
You got an answer.
Inhale, exhale.
You find comfort in this voice.
You find there is a choice.
The bindings loosen.
Your freedom is near, safety is here.
Inhale, exhale.
Breathe.

Ice

There is a coldness that has grown inside me,
a numbness,
frost that is slowly flowing through my veins,
freezing all the warmth that exists in my heart,
extinguishing every fire with a breath of death;
leaving me very cold, my temperature so low.
I wonder if I'm dead inside.
My stare is an icicle, sharp as a knife, and deadly if the blade falls.
The chill is so deep; I feel my bones cracking.
My body aches, and I feel I am slipping into a deep sleep.
But the slumber is restless.
And no matter how much my Sun shines on me,
I can't wake up.
The snow keeps building.
Even if it melts,
I'm not sure my Sun would like what is beneath,
and I would drown.

Embers

This calming voice.
Her mind challenging.
She is a shade of color I don't recognize.
I don't poke embers,
but you fuel a fire in me.
I want this blaze to ignite.
I want to feel this warmth.
Setting this gloom aflame,
a fight I demand,
but you don't need me to stand.
You hold your ground,
taking your battle stance.
A dance you lead,
feeding and fueling this fire,
concurring and taking control.
I should have followed your steps;
my instincts for my love took over.
I don't want to be this way.

Haunt

I am alone in the dark.
The only presence
is this shadow,
a demon stalking me,
gripping my throat,
watching me gasp for air,
letting go...
and choking me again.
He is not tormenting me,
it is his nature,
a disease
plaguing his body, mind.
He is destruction,
a ghost,
haunting me.
But even that apparition,
chasing me in my nightmares...
I would rather this phantom,
than to not have him at all.

Broken

Bent and broken this pain I swallow.

Hollow and empty, living in this shell.

Save me, save me.

Take me away from this insidious nightmare.

I don't have a care in this world.

I want to bleed these feelings away.

Pain and anger possess me.

Exorcise my body and soul,

devour me whole.

Save me.

Take me.

Destroyed and desperate;

not a care in this world,

oblivious to this oblivion,

absent and powerless.

Take me, take me.

I want to feel nothing...

but you make me feel everything.

This first touch wakes me.

You saved me.

Heavy

I felt a drop of heavy rain.
I looked up and saw the downpour.
Being bathed in thick warm rain drops,
I wanted to stand there forever.
Even with a gloomy grey sky,
it was a weight I didn't mind.
Drenched, soaked,
I would have let it drown me.
Seeing people panic,
running for cover,
I stood there and never wanted to leave.
I felt at peace in the storm.

Who Are You?

Who are you today?
Is this my Love?
Is this the Angel?
Is this the Shadow?
Is this the Devil?
Who are you today?

Rhapsody

This Rhapsody has finally ended.
Descended from an odyssey.
Not flawless, but beautiful.
Connecting us by bridges.
A history that will be defended.
Offended some and may bring contention,
yet flourishing our lives through conversation.
Nourishing our minds, enriching our souls;
not flawless, but beautiful.

Ballet

She's a force of nature.

Something strong and ambiguous.

Intelligent, humorous, stunning, kind.

She moves in a dance and motion I've never experienced.

I try to keep step,

but she is always a step ahead.

I'm stumbling on my feet like a baby,

maybe one day I can keep up.

She inspires me to enjoy this journey;

a tourney that I don't want to win,

but just keep pace,

hold my seat.

Her soul traces my heart.

I can feel her touch,

even a million miles away.

My heart beats with a new rhythm

in tempo with yours.

SEASONS

Summer

This Summer's Sun is hot.
The long, thick rays touch my body,
drawing beads of sweat
as boiling as his touch is.
My body shivers.
This Summer bird's voice carries,
singing a song that is pleasing to the ears.
These rays dig deeper.
This Sun keeps shining on me,
never looking away.
I melt.
It starts to rain.
These warm drops coat my skin.
The ecstasy I feel makes me tremble.
The rain turns into a river.
I enjoy this flowing sensation
covering my body.
I like the way this Sun shines down on me,
never blinking.
His light shines just for me.
This game lasts all Summer.

Fall

These leaves are a brilliant, vibrant red,
just on the edge of falling.
The wind blows in many directions.
Sometimes, I wish it would blow just right,
snap my stem, so I could float to the ground.
These changing Seasons are again exhausting.
I feel the weather changing.
I feel this cool breeze and know what's coming.
Waking up and feeling these tears of dew.
Behind these grey clouds,
the Sun seems to hide lately.
These days are usually few but increasing.
I miss my Spring... the beautiful bouquet,
her smell...
She can make the darkest, coldest Winter snow melt with her touch;
make a wilting rose spring to life again;
make a frozen lake flow.
These roots are planted deeply inside of me.
These branches are reaching out
and starting to spread.
This red leaf is weighing very heavy today.
I miss my wild Spring flower
dancing in her field of poppies.
She is so addictive.

Winter

This Spring is flowing too strong.

These leaves have turned brown and have fallen.

I am turning into a dark frozen Winter.

Seasons like these pass slowly and visit too often.

It is hard to live inside of me.

My mind is a wasteland of noise and random thoughts.

On days like these, I do not see a Spring coming.

No flowers bloom in this place.

There is no heat from the Summer.

I am freezing... so cold.

I am Ice.

This permafrost is spreading quickly.

I am numb.

I hate these constant changing Seasons.

They are tiring, exhausting, and unfortunately...

uncontrollable.

Spring

I yearn for this time of Season,

...this Spring.

Seeing these red roses bloom...

She is always far and time is often short.

This Season is my favorite time.

When she greets me and those soft petals touch my skin,

when her stem entangles me, wraps me up, squeezes me tightly,

she makes my spirit shine like the brightest Sun.

She makes all the grey disappear.

Her scent entrances me.

Her eyes and that smile steal all my sadness.

It's hard not to have this Spring all year round,

not to see my wild Spring flower dancing.

But these are my Seasons and they come, and they go.

Knowing that I will see my Spring again,

makes all the cold Winters,

dying and falling leaves,

worth her short visits.

She is always distant.

But that Spring is worth every second of the cold,

harsh, frozen moments in time when she is gone.

I love my Spring

...and she knows.

CANVAS

Canvas

Looking at your face I see blue.
I can taste your sadness.
When we part, this color always envelopes you.
I've noticed that your numbness is going away.
You are starting to feel, you have defrosted,
and I'm not sure how you are handling it.
I think it's overwhelming for you.
You are starting to wake up to this blue.
My color is grey.
When we part, a dark cloud follows me.
Everything is in black and white.
You are the only artist that can bring color to my canvas.
When we are together, it is a beautiful masterpiece.
Rare... there is nothing else like us.
I miss you and those slow strokes
when we start painting.
Soft and perfect blending.
We take our time, like we have forever.
A perfectly chosen palette.
These colors are organic.
We paint this canvas with ease.
The result is more than satisfying.
Every touch, no matter how faint or deep,
fills this canvas with a picture we will never forget.
But there is always that last kiss,
when I see your blue and my color drains
to a blank canvas.

Blue

I saw your color change again to blue.

My canvas became empty, void of color.

Any color brushed on your canvas fades quickly.

The brightest color you paint on my canvas turns to black and white.

The artist doesn't seem to matter.

The last grain of sand has dropped.

Watching it fall reminds me of what little time I have left.

Watching drops of emotion stroke your cheek

changed the painting that we were.

It was a masterpiece,

but time degraded this canvas;

this painting is deformed now,

an unrecognizable mess of what was once a beautiful piece of art,

unlike anything the world has ever seen.

Grey

Grey clouds and black sky.

My canvas is a blank slate.

The art is there, but I see right through it.

The world is a blending of darkness,

dimmed stars, new moon, and no Sun to rise.

No light reflects on this canvas to bring out the colors that were once

painted.

I hope that we can paint again.

I hope that the canvas gets filled.

I want to see my art brilliant, and shining,

like the silver Angel she is.

Sea of Blue and White

Floating through a sea of blue and white,
disembodied and weightless.
The storm cleared and I see my Heaven.
Entering through these Pearly White Gates, I see my Angel.
It feels like it's been forever.
Her wings are as beautiful as I remember.
Her halo is shimmery, bright silver.
Her touch brings me to tears.
God, how I've missed her cool, soft skin,
just as I remember.
A smile that can chase away any demon.
A scent that fills the room and brings comfort.
Her eyes are amber.
Through those windows, I can see her soul,
and her harp is strumming a tune just for me.

Night and Stars

Your paint is spilling onto me,
draining the canvas once more.
Swirls of blue with distorted stars.
Depressed silver and dimmed golds that were once bright
but shine no more.
I see distance in the hills and dark shadows over our Home.
Our silence, again, feels like death.
A night that seems like it will never end.
A still sky, motionless,
but in the motions of our painting is a flowing river of pigments.
Some bright and vigorous, others are dark and cold.

BLACK WIDOW

Sea of Silk

The spider has spun her web.
I'm caught and feeling dread.
Staring with its many eyes,
to poison me and watch me die.
So long since I've been free,
trapped in this silky sea.
Wanting a quick release,
soon I will be deceased.
I feel it on my skin.
Bite me, taste me, take me in.
Venom fluent in my vein,
I convulse calling her name.
She's the last I want to see
before I go to sleep.
Waiting for life to drain,
to be free from these strains.

Latrodectism

You are a beautiful creature,
all black, except an hourglass of red.
Your silver web is enticing, to say the least.
Many get stuck and beg for death,
but your poison is a familiar taste;
people don't die from it,
but their screams make you hide.
All the noises in your head from the meals you've devoured,
leaving you hanging by a single thread.
Soon you will be stuck in the web you spun,
and you will become the refection.

Widow Spider

I am a Black Widow.
I am not aggressive by nature,
but my bite drips with venom.
When you pluck the threads of my web,
my smooth silk sings an abrasive tune.
I will grab you and my fangs will dig deep.
You won't die from latrodectism,
but my bite will leave you paralyzed,
your muscles aching, shaking, and begging for death.
The pain will leave you changed forever.
Left with a black heart unable to love completely.

FEAR

Disappeared

What will you do if I disappear?
I hate the thought of not being near.
When nowhere you go feels like Home.
Where all the roads are empty where you roam.
When every corner you turn, you see my face.
Everywhere you travel, you feel out of place.
When nothing in life taste the same.
Every nightmare you scream my name.
When you can't feel the warmth of my touch.
My skin next to yours, and kisses, and such.
What will you do when I'm not around?
I hate the thought of you being so down.
When nothing in life brings you joy,
because everything you love gets destroyed.
When the only water you taste are tears.
This, my Love, is my deepest fear.

Apparition

I was visited by that apparition.
I'm wondering is this a premonition.
Am I in death and haunting her?
That look on her face is pure fear.
Lost, alone, and haunted when I'm gone.
Her life has ended, but she still lives on.
Her loneliness and emptiness is hell.
She rose high, flew, soared, and fell.
Left without my arms to catch her.
No more love to rain upon her.
No more of my warm hands to caress her at night.
This ghost keeps haunting me in my sleep.
I'm starting to think her loss of me is what I see.
In the dark, in my death, it's her screams.
I hear in my dreams, never-ending sobs,
drowning in a sea of her own tears.
A ghost of the woman I knew and loved,
forever haunted by my absence.

Distorted

Last night I dreamed of you.
It was hard to see you.
You were distorted, your voice cracked.
I couldn't hear your message,
but I think I understood.
I could say anything,
write a million verses,
but your visage kept fading.
I already felt alone before you disappeared.

Remnant

This distance between us
is turning into nightmares.
I hear your screams in my dreams.
I feel your fear when I'm awake.
I live your sadness.
I feel you falling apart.
The cuts from the pieces of your heart are deep.
This puzzle is crumbling faster than I can solve it.
Some pieces are so shattered, they don't fit anymore.
I'm frantically trying to put you back together.
I'm missing parts of this picture.
This jigsaw is incomplete.
My hands are numb.
I'm fumbling, dropping you.
I need to solve this, but every piece is deformed.
They are melting in my hands.
I won't give up.
I'm saturated with you.
After you disappear, all that's left is this stain;
just a reminder, a remnant, a memory.

Broken in Half

My heart feels like it's broken in half.

This pain is overbearing.

Today has been the worst.

I feel you slipping away.

I feel like there is only a trace of you left.

I've never wanted to hold on to something so tightly,

but I feel like no matter how hard I hold you,

you are still disappearing.

The image of you in that dream haunts me.

I've never felt so sad in my life.

I really miss you.

I love you so much.

Dreams and Nightmares

Dreams and nightmares.

Seeing a mirage in the distance.

Is this real? A hallucination?

An open world, so much to explore.

A beautiful landscape left up to our imaginations.

My mind has dried to a desert.

So much space but buried deep in the sand.

Feeling abandoned.

A cast off.

I still see you... a blur,

a shimmering image that is fading.

You have never departed,

but we are parted.

My mind is a buried tomb.

Ancient thoughts and feelings are coming to surface.

Should you keep uncovering this mastaba,

or bury it deeper in darkness?

Overthinker

As I build this tower,

and shower you with feelings I never knew existed,

the void is still there.

I feel so alone.

Every day is just droning on.

Maybe you can't fill this emptiness.

Since we've met, I feel you around me all the time.

I don't know if you are filling my heart or digging a hole.

I don't know if you are freeing me or taking control.

Is this a game, maybe it's more of the same?

Maybe it's just me overthinking,

digging my own grave.

Maybe I can't be saved.

Maybe I'm just not used to being loved like this.

Maybe I should just breathe, relax, and absorb this.

You really are my world.

I think I'm okay with that.

Fear

I have a new presentiment,
a sentiment that isn't nostalgic.
Sometimes fear takes over,
anxiety digs deep and covers me.
She blankets me in feelings I never knew existed,
panic, agitation, consternation,
love, longing, wanting, needing.
But with these fears, I feel love that I never knew existed.
Maybe it's a fear of deserving this love.
Maybe it's a fear of losing this.
Maybe it's just fear of not knowing.

One Day

The Sun was shining,

then the grey clouds rolled in.

I hear the rain tapping,

the thunder screaming.

Quickly, the weather changed.

I think it's going to flood.

The day turned to night.

The Sun set.

Will it rise again?

It seems like it's always pouring.

Beautiful dawns are less frequent.

Lightning flashing, crashing in my head; it's blinding.

The storm is deafening.

The noises drown out everything.

My surroundings are black and white.

Shudders of exposure. Strobes of truth.

This maelstrom might take me down.

If I can only weather the storm,

just till the morning.

I have to see the light shine again.

One day at a time.

Isolation

I don't know the direction the wind is blowing.

All I know is, it's cold and unforgiving.

The snow building on the ground.

The Sun covered with dark clouds.

The feeling of isolation.

The world watching with gloomy eyes.

Blurred vision in a storm that won't break.

Far too much heartache.

How many mistakes can be forgiven?

How many times can we freeze to death and be revived?

Time... is starting to slip by.

I wonder, will the weather clear?

Breathless

These hands are scarred.

It's hard to wrap myself around this.

I feel like I'm suffocating.

You breathe life into me,

but you also take my breath away.

I don't like losing control.

I see old dreams creeping in;

these thoughts I have forgotten,

these feelings I've blocked.

You know me, you see me, hear it in my voice.

I've built a wall, lifted my shield.

These layers are wilting.

There is nothing that can stop this storm.

I feel the electricity, I know lighting is going to strike.

This flower might die before it can bloom.

Nosferatu

Your fangs dig deep,

draining me.

It's satisfying,

but you leave me dying.

If I don't see you soon, I feel everything will wash away.

You keep hiding, and I keep this tattoo on my sleeve.

You know what I mean.

Maybe I can't predict the weather...

but you are my sunrise,

and I wait for that daybreak.

Thief

Running, being chased,
making haste, trying to be safe.
Tripping, falling for this devil.
Leveled, tilling my own grave.
Chiseling my own tombstone;
always alone, fading in this shade.
There you are again; screaming,
incoherent, iridescent.
Haunting me.
So cold.
You have a tight hold.
Stealing my soul.
I need you.

Chaos

My heart bleeds.

This pain brings me to my knees.

My armor is rust, falling apart,

shedding this demeanor.

Falling down, lost and broken,

my soul cracks, my mind impotent;

distant, pushing down this affliction,

my spirit burns and catches on fire.

Beautiful and rhythmic, I start to sway,

turning into motion, captivated, entranced,

spiraling through this chaos.

Please exhale this noise.

I'm so numb, feeling empty and useless.

I feel like I need to walk.

What suffering am I causing?

My patience is wearing thin.

And my heart is grating.

This is testing me,

pushing my limits.

Is this worth it?

Undertow - Swell

This wave folds

and the impact of the crash takes me down

beneath this dark undertow.

This feeling of loss and breathlessness... it's terrifying.

As I struggle to make it to the surface,

I know you will be there, waiting.

It's the one thing that gets me swimming.

Trying desperately to breathe again.

You are the only one who makes this tired body and mind function;

my breath of fresh air, my breath of life.

You make these numb muscles, feel again.

You make this racing mind, calm.

This missing feels like death.

It's crippling, but knowing that you are swimming towards me,

and that you will take my hand,

makes this numbness worth it.

Undertow - Surge

Swept again... taken by the undertow.

This time, I don't want to reach for your hand.

I feel calmness in these dark waters.

I don't want to take a breath.

There is comfort knowing you are here,

but at this point I have no fear.

I miss us, but I don't want to drag you to the bottom.

I will go down alone instead of taking you with me.

I know you will go down to save me...

That is real love.

In the Dark

I live in the dark,
watching the night sky.
I love the bright stars,
brilliant colors, crisp and clear.
You bask in the Sun,
but it casts a silhouette.
In the brightest light,
you are a shadow,
shrinking and growing.
Depending on the position,
never knowing where the shade is;
no one can get a glimpse of your visage.
My world looks like death;
your side looks like living.
Neither of us are truly alive.
The leaves on my tree
died and have fallen;
the leaves on your tree are vibrant.
But we haven't really lived.
We are so close but always distant.
There's always a question...
Is the Sun rising, or setting?

Falling

All I want is to have time.

I don't have much.

The little bit I do have,

I need to spend it with you.

I watch the clock for a reason.

These Seasons, dying and falling leaves,

are rapidly fading... and the sun is burning out.

A flickering candle in a dark room.

At any moment a light breeze will extinguish the minutes I have left.

I'm not sure why I met you,

but maybe I need someone to hold my hand,

walk with me, guide me through the darkness,

make sure that when the sand runs out,

I find my way to a peaceful rest.

It's a hard thing to ask and even harder thing to mask.

QUALM

Endure

What do you have to endure
to be with me?
I see and feel it all.
How much can you bend before you break?
How far can we push this envelope?
The sacrifices you have to make...
Is this a mistake?
You are strong,
but how much can you take?
Hell, how much can I?
As I sigh and watch you drift into your duties,
all this time is passing us by...
I've tried to express my love.
I've written a million words.
You have heard every one,
every syllable.
I see you everywhere.
You are everything to me.
As much as you fill my heart,
I feel empty.
Sometimes, a lot of the time.

Unresolved

I've noticed a change in you,
an extra sadness seeping through,
emotions unresolved,
things that need to be solved.
I'm here, I'm going to stay.
I'm never going to run away.
I just don't want to be in the way,
but I feel your heart is going astray.
I would sacrifice myself
if it meant you could be happy.
Maybe the wrong things are being taken off the shelf.
You told me to make a list.
It's a short one.
I have a ton of things weighing me down;
you are not one of them.
However, a part of you is on that enumeration.
I feel grounded when we talk.
To walk with you in life is Heaven.
At the same time, you are one of those things I can't change.
By change, I mean I want to help you,
I want to make you better.
I want to heal you,
but I think only time can do that.
And we have forever.
Thinking of you, always.

Tender

This fire burned intensely and hot.
The tenderness of this tinder
flickered and burned like brush during the Summer heat.
It was wild and will burn forever in my heart.
But my whispers in the wind are too much.
My every thought is written on paper;
read and set on fire.
When it's extinguished, it will remain a memory.
This lake of fire
won't freeze from your touch,
but will be put out by the few tears you cry,
and will dry in a new sunrise,
a new day.
The sun will shine again,
but my light won't be the rays that touch your skin.
It will be a new Sun,
and I hope you can dance again.
I hope that smile spreads across your face...
That one that shines in my memory,
that smile that I can't conjure with my words;
not anymore...
I've never failed so miserably.
You told me once, you made a wish...
I just blew out the candles of a dream,
and my wish was happiness for you.

Unforgiving

This demon is riding me, animated.

She keeps me held, tied down,

Immobile, still; and she's unforgiving.

A succubus, draining my existence.

I'm lost and can't see my way through.

But my love for her makes me stay true.

She is a dream,

also a nightmare you don't want to wake up from,

because if you do, she is gone;

a figment, a mirage, a whisper,

a ghost that haunts you, unforgiving;

forever.

It's a feeling that is new, unfamiliar.

But this caterpillar will turn quickly into a butterfly;

and the beauty is tempting,

makes you lose control,

may take your soul.

I give in.

Take me.

I need you, I want you.

I'm yours...forever.

Watermelon

When you landed on this Island, it grew fruit.

An abundance of delight you could chew.

Slowly this fruit spoiled and turned.

The Sun disappeared, and the earth grew cold.

You curled up tightly in your cocoon.

One night you turned into a butterfly

and took flight.

You flew far and high with your beautiful wings.

Blizzard

The Winter has come again. Unpredictably.

The coldest Season yet.

I feel the absence of our nature,

the singing of the birds,

even the howls of the wolves.

This is... something I fear more than the deadliest beasts.

This blizzard is blinding, keeping me in my shelter,

unable to travel, to hunt, to gather, to live.

She is trapped, buried.

The distance is still the same,

but the journey is more treacherous.

Our fingertips seem like they can touch,

like we are right there.

Even if our fingers touched,

even if my arms grabbed you,

and I held you as tightly as I could...

what would that sensation feel like?

Would you recognize me?

Would we be the Persons we knew?

Or would it bring our coldest Season yet?

Even if the Sun rose and burned brilliant, sizzling,

like the hottest Summer's day...

would it be enough to melt the snow that has piled up?

Enough for us to survive the rest of this Season,

and see our Spring again?

Or will this be the Fall of the most beautiful years of our lives?

Part of Me

My infinite patience.

My enchanting charisma.

As you lay here immobile,

I control you.

I take from you what I will.

Your breath, my hands gripping like a vice.

Your blood on this bed of roses.

Red petals floating down, soaking the ground.

I wish I could see your expression,

but this poison makes you my possession.

Your tears taste like fear.

Your cries are music to my ears.

The faint sounds of struggle, your breath restricted.

The smile on my face widens.

My grip on you tightens.

This pleasure, the ecstasy,

as the light fades in your eyes.

I will always remember you.

Just like the others.

You will always be a part of me.

Cycle

I am just another Star,

shining and fading in an immense universe.

All these Stars gravitate around you.

You can't help but take them in.

You accept these Suns as they crash and burn.

You are constantly losing something.

I worry that you don't have much left to lose, or to gain.

Like someone explained recently,

the space and dimensions have no shape.

It's a viscous cycle that we put ourselves through.

But like this person said,

the cycle continues,

and we can keep showing up

or just fade away.

Weathered

So many pieces missing.

Everything we've loved is disappearing,

one after another.

I am a secret.

I feel like I am a page in a book of secrets;

something you can turn to

when you feel the need,

when you feel like I need it.

You are a page in my weathered book.

Mostly beautiful clouds and sunny days,

but today is grey, and the rain is pouring.

This page is so saturated,

I can't read it.

If I touch it,

it will shred, fall apart between my fingers.

There are pieces I won't be able to mend.

No amount of adhesive will heal it.

So, I should close my book,

and wait...

Promises

Promises made and broken.

Words said and unspoken.

Things meant, and things dreamt.

Life lived, and life tried.

Hearts mended, and hearts died.

Living in a world, or stuck in a box.

So many random thoughts.

So many there, so many gone.

So many things went wrong.

Roads taken, and dead ends.

So many enemies, so many friends.

Floating on clouds, or buried in ground.

This viscous cycle that spins round.

Lift yourself up, or stay down.

Dust

Prying open my mind.

All these grains of sand and time.

A dust storm, blinding, no sense of direction.

Every particle is sprinkled on you.

It is why you walk through this dust devil.

You want to know, but so do I.

Your mind is a buried tomb.

You say I am your Person, your confidant.

But this archaeologist is digging with his hands.

What Person am I, if I can't even slide the sarcophagus door
and discover?

This path we walk on is covered.

I am so tired of sweeping the dust just for it to be covered again.

I am blind in the eyes of this storm.

Kettle

The kettle is boiling;
red hot and steaming.
Broken dreams, empty promises.
This roiling is foiling.
I hate this disturbance.
Not sure who set this fire;
maybe I did.
This explosion is inevitable,
unpredictable.
This hot spring
can spill on anyone at anytime.
I wish I could turn the heat down,
at least to a simmer.
This kettle has been on the flame too long.
If it keeps burning, I will evaporate.

Load

I'm floating on this cloud
high above the ether.
Everything is so loud.
My ears ringing, it's deafening.
I can't fly, I can't soar anymore.
I'm dipping, and diving, and stumbling, and crying, and fading away.
I'm having trouble reaching you.
With every silence, my words go still;
frozen and choking on every syllable.
I'm not sure which glass to fill.
You are hiding but are still visible.
This dream is fading into a nightmare
as I stare at this ceiling, paralyzed.
Motionless, emotionless, yet so many emotions.
This glass is so full.
I know what I need to do, but I don't have the strength.
My body is aching; I feel like my mind has done a thousand reps.
I have this spotter helping me lift this load,
but I think this weight is too heavy for us.

Threshold

My threshold is a wall.

Thick stone, solid Granite pillars, and very tall.

It's almost impossible to climb.

Lately, it's crumbling down.

I'm starting to see the weakness in this structure.

I'm seeing the seams come apart.

I'm seeing the limits.

I would rather be blinded by the light reflecting from these pale,

white, marble bricks.

I would rather not notice the fissures in the stone.

I'm not sure if it's worth maintaining this Home.

There are so many rooms in this castle.

There are so many ghosts that haunt these halls.

I'm not sure where I belong.

I feel like I'm just a visitor,

a guest, good company until my time is spent.

Everything looks so familiar.

I love running my fingers down these walls,

I love the scent, the perfume.

But there is something in the air,

something turning, rotting, like death.

I love my Home, but I'm not sure I live here.

Push It

I've tried.

I've hunted for this love.

I don't know how it died.

The closer I get, the more you push and shove.

I hope he can dry the tears from your eyes.

I hope he gives you something I'm not.

I hope what you have with him never stops.

The closer you get, I hope you grab and hold.

I told you,

I would walk if you could be happier in another's arms.

I couldn't hold tight enough,

or maybe my grip was too strong.

I guess I don't know my own strength.

Maybe I held on just too long.

Maybe the reach and length is too far.

Maybe the scars are too deep.

My glass is full and overflowing.

Every drop in this glass is a part of you.

Maybe that's why I failed.

I'm here, just reach out and touch my hand.

But I don't think you need me anymore.

Charon's Obol

I'm so lost.

I do wonder, what's the cost?

My mind, my body, my soul, my heart.

Is it worth the toll?

You are in control.

Is this too much?... no.

But I deserve more.

My love is not cheap.

I do not give it freely.

My love is a rare currency.

When I love, I love with all of me.

I am not in debt to anyone.

My affection is not bankrupt.

I am rich when it comes to romance.

It does hurt when you can't even toss me a coin.

Chess

I feel like there are too many pieces on the chessboard.
I'm just a Pawn, protecting my Queen.
I will sacrifice myself if I have to,
there is no question about that.
Sometimes, it feels like with every move forward,
you are always two moves ahead.
I feel like I'm playing a game I can't win,
but I will never tip over my King.
I will see where this match takes me.
Maybe the other player is distracted.
I know I'm overthinking my move.
If I concentrate enough I can see the big picture.
I feel like I've been playing this game for a lifetime,
yet I don't remember how it's played.
I'm patient as long as the other player is true.
The clock keeps ticking, but I'm not sure whose move it is.

Muddy Waters

I visit this River often.

I dive deep.

But each time the dirt clouds these waters,

I can't see the bottom anymore.

I climb out each time not feeling myself,

caked in mud and feeling like filth.

I used to love being soaked in this pool,

drowning in you, feeling you all around me.

But now I feel trapped, neck deep in you;

I can't take a breath anymore without inhaling water.

This water is thick and viscous.

This quicksand isn't the Summer River

I remember.

With each dive, this River is getting smaller.

The height of this fall is elevating.

I don't want to play here anymore.

This Summer has turned to Winter.

The joy I once felt

doesn't outweigh the pain.

I can't swim here anymore.

Waiting for the Storm to Break

Waiting for the storm to break, but the rain has gone dry.

Another grey day, but I am still here.

Just a part of me, a drizzle.

A light breeze inside a hurricane.

I am the eye of the storm,

watching the destruction as it unfolds.

Hearing the thunder and watching the flashes of lightning,

I am calm.

Dead eyed,

watching us being torn apart;

I will not pick up the pieces.

I am calm in the eyes of the storm.

When the Seasons Stop

At the end of a mile.

The last stretch of the road.

The ending of our journey.

It was a beautiful road trip.

All the changing Seasons,

cold, hot, beautiful red leaves.

I feel like I'm always driving,

but the destination is never in sight.

All these dead ends;

I don't think I can turn around.

The volume on the radio is low,

the stations are just static.

No sad songs, no happy songs;

just nothingness.

Courage in the Dark

I woke up in mourn.
I heard the rain falling down;
no light visible.

The curtains drawn tightly.
The darkness is comforting.
The silence welcomed.

The noise disappeared.
I am finally alone.
I am in control.

I am not afraid,
just present in the moment.
Finally no fear.

Courage in the dark.
I'm cold, empty, and frozen.
Beware of my love.

Glass

I think the glass is empty.

The sand has run out.

Time has run its course.

This is the worst moment...

Letting go.

It doesn't matter who says the words;

the wounds are just as deep,

the scars will linger forever.

You can't flip the hourglass,

you can't turn back time.

There is no rhyme, poem, nor word

that can resurrect us.

If I stay, we will both be lifeless;

I don't deserve that,

neither do you.

Because I truly love you, I have to let you go.

MY FIGHT

Depression

This demon,
this beast
creeping in
takes my joy,
steals my self-worth,
changes me.
This misery,
this puppet master,
pulling my strings.
This unseen stalker
chasing me,
making my scars bleed again,
dragging me deep into the void.
Hidden but always present;
turning my sunsets
to dark emptiness.
This creature lurks in the deepest depth of my mind
but always seems to find the surface.
This is depression.

Manic

Not sure which mask I'm wearing today.

Looking in the mirror, the face is the same.

The way I feel day to day, hour to hour.

It's weather that changes so often.

I don't know what to wear.

I try to take the masks off,

to see clearer, to feel normal,

but I have to put the new ones on,

just to protect myself from the others.

Layers and layers of suffocating endless images that are me,

and not me at the same time.

Only a portion can shine through,

yet sometimes all of it does.

It's blinding, confusing, dangerous...

It's manic.

Wild Fire

This depression is contagious,
It is spreading like a brush fire.
I see it in the eyes of my loved ones,
I hear it in their voices.
The more I feel this heat, the more I burn.
The more I burn, the more this fire spreads.
I try to keep this contagion down,
but I am failing.
When I am down, everyone feels it.
I am the one who has to be hard as Granite,
but this lava is consuming me,
melting me down to nothing.
I try to suppress this blaze,
but I can't see through the haze.
This smoke... it's blinding me, suffocating.
The more I feel it, the more I know I will lose.
I have to snap out of this.
I have to put this wildfire out.
But it's spreading fast.
It might not be able to be contained.
I feel like Patient Zero.
Unfortunately for my loved ones,
they need me to be the Hero.

Frostbite

This ice I'm skating on is wearing thin.
I see myself frozen beneath.
Frozen tears, like icicles; voice cracked.
My breath lost and feelings abstract.
Teeth clenched, I don't know where to begin.
At the same time, I'm burning
red hot, and melting everything,
setting my world on fire.
These unfurled emotions are dire.
There seems to be no direction,
no safe step to run from this dejection,
to burn or to freeze, either way, I can't breathe.

Conflict

I don't think I will ever know peace.

I will never be free.

These shackles.

These chains; always holding me.

These bindings wrapped so tight.

These ropes knotted and hanged,

dangling from branches of despair.

Always alone.

Silence is noise.

Surrounded by faces I don't recognize.

A mirror with a reflection of disguise.

Loud rabble of language I can't understand.

The noise.

The silence.

Demons on my heels.

Running in quicksand.

Struggling. Sinking.

Fleeting hope. Lose of courage.

Every escape lands me in this cell.

Again,

and again,

and again.

Fear the Night

This shadow stalks me.
This nightmare,
resurrected,
reborn every night.
This phantom chasing me.
I can't escape you.
This recurrence is tiring.
There is no light here;
no stars to guide me.
Just thick mist of fear and sadness,
dark and terrorizing.
I'm blind, but I feel you.
That chilling hand reaching.
I feel my back numbing;
I inhale and choke,
breathing in this smog
of hate and anger.
You are so furious.
I'm so tired.
But I fear the night,
closing my eyes,
waking in that dark place again,
with you stealing my breath,
with your cold hands around my neck.

Mercy

Being held down

Can't take a sip of air

Gripped so tight

Entangled

Trapped

Motionless

I need a breath

I need motion

Not to run

To stand up

Fight or flight

I can't do either

Please release me

Just let go

Mercy

Stone

I have to put on a smile,
To show I'm okay.
But these tears fall when they're away.
I can't leave, I can't stray.
I'm all they have, so I have to stay.
I found this new diamond.
She's so bright and shining.
Her heart is right here with me.
I call her "Home," it's where I belong.
It's where I want to be.
I can reach out, feel it beat.
Before my fingers grip,
it dissipates, vanishes.
It's hard to concentrate.
The sky is falling.
Hell is calling.
I reap what I sow,
pay the devil what I owe.
Life's out of control.
Set ablaze, but I'm so cold.
I'm all alone.
My heart is encrusted in stone.

Unknown

I'm feeling so lonely today.

Isolated, in a very dark room.

The pain is starting to increase.

It's like a loud, steady ringing in my head.

I don't want to be here.

I don't want to be anywhere.

I want to just turn everything off.

I usually just let things unfold and be what they are,

but for some reason, I'm scared.

It's not a feeling I'm used to.

I'm not sure why I feel this way, but something is going to happen,

something that I'm not prepared for.

I just don't know.

Chills

I lost my breath.
The pressure is building in my chest,
spreading across my muscles,
from my heart to the tips of my fingers.
The pounding is literally deafening.
My heart slows as soon as this episode starts,
but I still can't catch my breath.
The pressure increases and the pounding starts again.
It stops as quickly as it ignites.
The pressure increases, numbness creeps across my arms.
I still can't breathe, I feel like I'm drowning,
and I can't swim,
my arms and the pressure in my chest prevent me from moving.
Just as quickly as it starts it disappears.
All that's left is an unsteady feeling in my chest.
Tired limbs and exhaustion.
All this happened and went away in seconds.

Day Turned to Night

This day was beautiful.

The bluest sky, white clouds painted in brilliant strokes.

The sun, an illuminated beacon, letting me know things are okay.

A cool breeze kissed my skin,

but suddenly, black clouds rolled in;

it started to pour.

The rhythm of the rain was heavy;

fast tempo pounding on my chest.

My shoulders tensed.

The pressure I felt was unbearable.

The thunder was crashing.

The lightning was blinding.

I was frightened.

This storm brewed into existence so quickly.

It usually leaves just as fast,

but this time it lingered.

Even drowning in this,

you were on my mind.

As always,

this storm passed,

but I'm still shaken.

You saved my life today.

Thank you.

Control

The anxiety today is paralyzing.

My depression is a flood, a hurricane.

I've never been so overtaken by emotions.

I've never lost control like this.

I can't have a single thought.

My mind is a blank slate,

yet so many visions and images flash by.

These tears are uncontrollable.

I want to breathe but hold my breath at the same time.

I want to run but need to be still.

I need to find a way to calm this storm.

I'm at a loss.

For the first time, I don't have an answer.

I feel so fucking helpless.

Monster

This is a living nightmare.
This anger is consuming me.
This disease is back again.
It laid dormant for years.
I try to stay away.
I don't want this to spread.
Appearing from nowhere,
this dark cloud floats over me,
cascading down, it envelopes me.
I can't see through the fog.
Now this monster morphs.
It's starting to rain;
these tears burn me.
As this fire slowly fades,
a voice keeps whispering...
"Tomorrow will be a new day.
Stay positive, stay strong.
This pain will go away."

My Demons

Celadora

Walking through this dark hallway,
my third eye has gone astray;
questing for that cellar door.
What have I been waiting for?

I feel it, shaking.
I need it, aching.
I feel it, gnawing.
It's tasting and calling.

Stumbling through this passageway,
my third eye begs me to stay.
My feet dragging across the floor,
desperate to find that rusty door.

What's beyond the cellar door?
Cross the threshold.
Beg for more.
What's behind that cellar door?
A taste of forbidden wine,
or dine with fine china white?
Anything to make life numb.
Losing myself as I succumb.

(Continued on next page)

I need something to make life blissful,
because ignorance will not do.
I need something to make life tasteful;
I pray my love will come through.

I feel its power.
I hear it louder.
I start to cower, it begins to devour.

Crawling through this entranceway,
my third eye blind and decayed.
My mind lost the war,
I'm searching for that fucking door.

What's behind the cellar door?
A threshold I can't ignore.
What's beyond the cellar door?
A golden crown to choke my throat,
or puff my life up in smoke.
Anything to make life numb,
killing myself as I succumb.

Reflection

I can't stand what you see.
Mirror, why are you judging me?

Mirror, show me the person you want to see.
This repugnant image isn't me.

Mirror, what crimes did I commit?
I seem to forget.
Mirror, I don't like this reflection.
Please forgive my transgressions.

I'm lost and chained, but I'm no slave.
Disappointed, but I'm okay.
Sometimes I'm lost in my mind.
Mirror, please don't hate me for my crimes.

This hole is very deep,
I've been working at it for weeks.
I keep digging.
Mirror, I keep digging.

I'm lost and chained, but I'm okay.
Tomorrow is a new day.
Sometimes I'm lost, but a bridge can be found.
Mirror, maybe tomorrow I'll come around.

(Continued on next page)

Souls will be lost if you break,
I can't make that mistake.
I hope to see a new Person soon.
This ship has sank before,
but I can swim, I can swim.

I need him, and I need her
and they need me.
I don't want them to be alone,
I just want to come Home.

Mirror, so fragile it scares me.
Mirror, so taunted it scares me.
Mirror, so tainted I can't see.
I'm no slave, I want to be free.
Mirror.

The Gavel

The gavel has fallen before I could speak.

The sound took my self-esteem.

My future turned dark and bleak.

This is a life sentence for me.

And after all this time in prison,

I now know this is a false conviction.

I'm not sure if I will ever get my freedom;

my mind will always be behind bars.

The judgement was passed too early,

I never stood a chance,

never had a stance.

These walls are transparent but thick as stone.

I've always felt alone,

ever since that hammer hit Home.

I'll never escape, never tunnel my way out of this cell.

Even if I do, I will always be seen this way.

I'm trapped in the chains I smithed.

Even though I have the key, it doesn't seem to fit.

It's a recurring nightmare;

maybe I deserve to be here.

I hope one day I can be free;

look at myself in the mirror.

Maybe I can finally see the person I know I am.

I guess only time will tell, and I have plenty of that.

Pattern

When things go wrong,
I dig this hole, I sing this song.
These blues are true,
self-inflicted,
unpredicted, but a pattern is shown.
I can't tackle this, the solution is unknown.
I need to own this responsibility.
These screaming voices are loud and clear,
full of uncontrollable emotions.
This opera of commotion hitting every note,
but the timing is out of sync.
As I sink and drown in this disturbance,
flooded by transference of dominating,
complicating drama,
I need to swim free of this trauma.
My soul, my memories, a ghost haunting me,
possessing me,
and taking over my body, my soul, my mind.
Freedom seems like a dream.
There is no team that can be assembled
to fight this struggle.
This black hole is a void, a problem that can't be solved.

War

Off to war, again.

Not sure how many casualties will be left behind.

I hope we win this time.

This war must be won.

So many lives depend on it.

Erased

Made you my possession,
one of my collection.
So many I keep in this place,
locked down, disappeared, with no trace,
erased and damaged, never to be the same.
These thoughts that race through my head
make me unsteady and very dangerous,
monstrous, untamed, and my feelings leprous,
distraught, rotting, and falling apart.
As I sift through this debris,
I know I will never be free.
These past and present addictions
are a lifelong transition, a never ending nightmare,
a consistent calculation,
a never ending problem.

Dark World

I need it.

I need that needle,

that pain.

That ink spreading across my skin.

Those scars staining me,

like an infection...

but I love it, I enjoy it.

The pleasure, the pain,

lets me know I'm still alive.

I deserve it, this punishment,

this hell I created for myself,

this dark world I built.

This universe is so vast.

Seems like I will never find my way out.

This is my threshold;

I can't cross it.

This dam is stacked so high,

tall as a mountain.

I keep drinking from this fountain.

I can't swim, I'm drowning.

But my thirst is never quenched;

my mouth is so dry.

I can't speak, my words choke me.

They scare me.

I stutter every syllable.

I keep stumbling.

What's your threshold?

Labyrinth

This addiction is killing me.

It's sucking the life out of me.

It's blinding me.

It's destroying me.

This paranoia is melting me.

For the first time in my life I'm scared.

I truly fear for what I can lose.

My dreams slowly turn to sand,

and blow away in the wind.

These grains are impossible to piece together.

This labyrinth is impossible to navigate.

I've tried and failed, countless times.

This repetitive behavior will be the death of me.

Saving this soul is a lost cause.

I will keep trying, but this war seems lost.

I may win a battle or two,

but these wins are few.

I'm tired.

These muscles are failing.

This mind is a jungle.

I choke and drown on these tears.

I wither and hide from these fears.

This battle continues, and I see no light, no way out, no sunrise.

I see nothingness.

Swamp

I'm blind in this fog,

I can't see shit.

Knee-deep in this bog,

I wonder is this it.

It's wet and cold;

I can't stop shaking.

Stomach is cramped.

This anxiety feels like death.

Will it always be this way?

Every time I open my eyes,

ten years later

feels like an eternity.

I guess this is my hell,

the place I have to stay.

Buried alive.

There has to be a branch,

fucking something to hold on to,

so I can pull myself out of this shit.

Waist-deep now and sinking fast.

Fuck this swamp.

I'm so fucking tired.

Downfall

Frozen and numb.

The sum of a lifetime of regret,

an avalanche tumbling.

I saw a light from this grave,

a savior from this downfall.

All I see and hear is blinding white noise.

This freezing snow buries me.

I wish I had anger to start a fire.

I wish I had tears to put out those flames.

I wish I had an elixir for my sadness,

bottled and ready to quench this thirst.

This mountain that has caved in on me.

This Granite that is impenetrable.

This uncontrollable desire to free myself

from this tomb.

I just need a hand to reach for; that one to pull me up.

I always do this alone,

but that light I saw, that gift,

just inches away...

I almost had a hold.

But maybe, I don't see the rope of hope tossed down for me,

from the ones who choose to be here.

This darkness, this numb feeling, keeps me from healing.

We both see that hand, and we are grasping for it.

Waterboard

Gargling, struggling.
It's been some time
since I wasn't treading water.
My hands are bound.
Stuck on this merry-go-round.
Stuck inside this bottle,
floating at sea.
This vantage point is just waves crashing into me,
pushing me back.
No paddles, just drifting.
These dripping droplets drown me.
It's a slow death.
Strangling, hanging.
It's been some time
since I wasn't in this noose.
Swinging, dangling,
my feet can't touch the ground.
How long will it take
for this bottle to overflow
and sink me to the bottom?
Endless surfing on this waterboard.

Indistinguishable

Here I am,
lost and heartbroken.
Can't breathe again, I'm choking.
My life's set ablaze.
All this smoke is filling my lungs, blinding me;
eyes filled with tears.
I can't dive any lower, crawl any slower.
Just adding fuel to this fire.
In dire need... of something.
Hungry, thirsty, but I need to put this liquid down.
Drowning so deep in this river.
I shiver at the thought
of how far I'm from my shore.
I can see it, I can feel the sand between my toes.
It is so far away.
I really need it, I really want it.
Always so close,
but I can't touch it.
So low, digging my own grave.
Can I ever be saved?
This grit is wearing me down,
sanding me to nothingness.
Unrecognizable.
Looking at this image,
so familiar, yet indistinguishable.

Cannibal

These thoughts consume me.
This cannibal, carnivorous,
creature, feeding on my vitality,
leaving me incapacitated.
This compression of mind and body,
leaves me dry and drained.
This stain on my soul can never be washed away.
This hole in my heart can never be filled.
This trill shaking my existence,
pieces crumbling and spread likes ashes,
never to return.
I can never be whole again.

Onward

This sword plunged deep,
but I don't feel the pain.
Just drained from these battles.
This fight is exhausting.
Onward.
Battle weary and starting to give up.
Should I pull this sword from me,
or lean in?
As the light fades from my eyes,
I don't feel sad but relieved.
Onward.
Bleeding out, I stare at my companions.
They fought for me, gave their lives.
I'm so tired, my muscles failing,
but I pull this sword from my wound and fight on.
It's worth it.
Onward.

MY REFLECTION

New Beginning

Here I am, back at the start.

Alone, as always.

Even the deepest lovers turn,

and I watch them fade into the shadows.

I've always said I'm too much to handle,

which is why I'm left with this mirror's image.

This mirage, blurred view, cracked glass,

broken shards that cut deep...

I don't feel the pain,

but I watch the red river flow and collect at my feet.

The pool is very deep,

but I can swim;

I always make it ashore.

These broken pieces always seem to fall into place.

Tardis

I am a time keeper.

I see every second, every minute disappear.

It is hard for me to feel joy.

I see the little bit of happiness I get fade away,

every second, every minute.

It is draining, and I am losing.

I wish I could live, exist,

but I've always felt like I am already gone.

I feel like there is so little sand in my hourglass.

I see every grain fall.

This coarse life I'm living is getting to me.

Every second, every minute.

Jester

I'm a jester, a trickster.

I like to have fun.

I'm also a ghost that will haunt and fester.

I'm happy and sad, laughing and crying.

Always in the rain, dancing with no umbrella.

A spider stuck in its own web, ready to consume itself.

A butterfly in an inescapable cocoon.

I'm always flying, but in slow motion.

I'm a juggler, but the balls I toss in the air

never come down for me to catch them.

I'm impatiently patient,

tamed but wild.

A wolf gnawing off its own paw.

A madman that is completely competent.

A caring person without a care in the world.

I Wonder

My mind is traveling,
lifting and floating.

Never sleeping, always dreaming, and never stops thinking.
I'm wondering again.

My mind is unraveling,
drifting and flowing.

Nightmares unfold, out of control, and never truly knowing.
I'm wondering again.

You are distracting.
I'm lost and unfocused.

Melting into a universe of unknown.

I feel alone in a crowd;
I feel surrounded in nothingness.

So much space in this mind of mine.
Yet still, I feel trapped in a corner.

I feel sad, hopeless, and my soul has been sold.
I'm wondering again.

My mind is retreating.
I'm back in that place.

I don't fear much but this place scares me.
I'm wondering, pacing and my mind is my prison.

Cravings

It seems like there is always something I desire.
A craving, this gluttony is deadly.
I haven't figured a way out of these appetites;
they are a part of me.
It doesn't matter how far I run,
they are always following.
Sometimes, these feeling leave me hollow;
this emptiness is an addiction of its own, in a way.
Maybe, I'm just addicted to not being okay,
no matter how much I want to be.
These feeling have come to the surface lately.
It's hard to exhale these dark waters filling my lungs.
I can't breathe.
The only breath I take is when you are near.
I don't mind, I get light when you are around.
You make me dig through this dirt,
experience these things I've blocked for so long.
I know you feel like you are a burden,
but I assure you, that is far from the truth.
I don't depend on you, I just want you.
I do need you sometimes, but not in the way you think.
You are my light, my Spring, and I'm glad you are around.
I hope you know.

Decomposed

Some things I keep just for me;
unfortunately they try to surface.
I have to work hard and bury them deep.
Right now, they are crawling all around me.
I can't capture them and I can't put them away.
These things are starting to show,
and I don't want you to see them.
My mind and my body are decomposing.
I'm so lost and I want to stay gone.
I feel like such a burden.
I wonder how much longer you can tolerate me.
I'm just feeling so low right now.
I'm not sure where I want to be.
The only thing I know is that I love you.
I want to be with you.

Careful

This mask you uncover.

This sword digs in slowly,

heavily inadvisable,

blood-smeared and smudged.

These words are usually misunderstood.

The motions of this ocean's waves are feared.

These fists start to fly.

Numbed by anger as they flew.

Dreaded as I release this sin,

I can't pace this fury; it rages.

I'm not here to play.

It has been a long hunt for my prey.

This cage is compound.

There's no amnesty in the dark ages; I'm bound.

Forbidden words they cut deep like a knife.

I'm shaken and fighting this madness in me.

I do mind you suggesting me to grovel.

That's not what you're here for.

Know who you're trying to feed on.

Seeing worlds you fashion are not really there.

Healing never comes to surface.

Or maybe some feathers don't grow back, that's what I've heard.

These are scars filled with strife; it's not death.

By letting this build and boil to rage,

I need to let this out; it's imperative.

I've been a part of many worries,

messages I've been sending.

This world is a nightmare; fucking horrible.

Start deleting; I hope things come back from the years I took.

Damaged

Damaged.

Lost and rambling.

Speaking every word that comes to mind.

Trying to wrap my head around life.

And I'm reaching.

Failing.

My grip has lost its strength.

My vocabulary rhymes at length,

but the words seem meaningless.

Empty and hollow.

I can't strike the right cord.

I can't sing the proper song.

The timing, and melody, escapes me.

Such a tragedy to be loved so much,

but not be able to love oneself.

It's the one that got away,

and it flew far;

I don't think I can catch it.

Fade Away (Little Bird)

I tried to fly
I lost my wings
Almost died

I tried to sing
I lost my voice
Almost cried

A song I can't sing
A vision I can't see
A voice tries to speak
A whisper I can't hear

The silence is deafening
Experience life-threatening
Wish this voice would fade
Fade away

I tried to fly
I lost my wings
Almost died

I heard a song
I saw a bird
And I cried

(Continued on next page)

A song I now hear
A vision that tempts me
A little bird bends my ear
A voice so damn clear

This wind is weighing
This voice is saying
I won't fade
Fade away

I learned I can fly
I learned I can see
Colors so vivid I fear
So beautiful, I shed tears

Today I found my way
A mystery solved
Today the skies were grey
I took flight, fought, and stayed

I soared high
I soared far
My wings grew back
I evolved

I didn't fade
I didn't fade
Fade away

Didn't fade
Fade away
I stayed

Horizon

I'm in the darkest moment.

I can't see any light right now.

There are so many stars in the sky,

but they keep blinking and fading.

I feel so alone.

I have so many beautiful things in my life.

I know the Sun is shining.

I know the sky is blue; I know the grass is green.

But I really can't see it,

I can't feel it.

I am not okay.

I have this Star.

She shines just for me.

She is always there.

No matter what her light reveals,

no matter what shadows are cast,

she is okay with me.

She sees things I don't see.

I know these things are there, but I can't accept them.

I've never been able to be my own Star.

I've never been able to shine light on myself.

I love her warmth, but I don't depend on it.

I'm so glad her light is bright and shines on me,

but I know it's my light that needs to shine;

I have to illuminate my own sky.

Maybe someday, I will rise over the horizon,

I will shed light on my world.

Maybe someday I will be okay.

Immaterial

I feel empty and irrelevant,
immaterial, disconnected.
My life has become desolate,
feeling dejected.

I've learned many lessons,
sessions that shaped me.
My life is still incomplete,
sweeping up life's debris.

I feel alone and distressed,
immobilized, anxious,
a shell of who I used to be,
an empty clone.

Rinse and Repeat

I can't rewrite the past,
but I can jot down the present.
These little notes in a book of our own.

I feel a long way from Home.
I feel lost and cold on these streets.
I'm scared things won't last.

If I lose you, I'll be lost forever.
I've never felt this way.
I hope I won't miss you.

This cycle seems to repeat.
The water is still, even as I struggle.
No ripples, no sound, just my breath.

The water in my ears, my lungs.
It's the only sound I hear.

Treacherous

I wear this skin.

This armor guards me.

You can't see what's within.

You stare at these eyes, these black holes.

No light can penetrate these orbs.

If I let you in, you would never be able to leave.

If you would see the things I've done,

you'd be trapped in this abyss,

this dark void of regret.

You think you know me,

but I only let a little blood seep through my pores.

Careful,

this blood is tainted.

Like acid, it will tear through the layers of your soul.

Like poison, it will spread through your body

and contaminate your mind.

Careful,

I wear this disguise.

This mask hides me.

You don't want to see who I am.

You glare at this darkness,

trying to get a glimpse.

The trap is set.

Don't let this curiosity cloud your judgement.

Tread carefully.

These caverns are deep and this maze is treacherous.

Deliverance

My tears are flowing like a river.

You feel like you need to be my deliverance.

But I am the only one who can cure my sadness.

You make me as happy as you can.

There is nothing more you can do to heal these wounds.

I am my own savior,

but right now, I can only crucify myself.

I hope I will rise soon, before my sun sets.

You are my light, but I feel like I am not yours,

not anymore,

and I am sorry.

I am really tried, but I am my own demon.

I need to exorcise myself before I am consumed.

My fears of being myself have taken a toll.

I'm not sure if I can afford it anymore.

I am doomed.

Unfamiliar

I looked in the mirror today,

I didn't recognize the person I saw.

Is that me?

These eyes are unfamiliar.

The face looks similar.

Who am I?

This mirror is cracked.

This reflection is distorted.

I have this fear crawling through my skin.

My courage is wearing thin.

Who am I?

This mirror is bleeding shards of glass.

Some of the pieces fit,

but this puzzle is a journey.

This deja vu is a curse.

This agitation is getting worse.

Who am I?

I feel like I have to hide.

I feel the people in the shadows.

I'm scarred and my skin is blistered.

Staring at this broken mirror, I whispered...

Who am I?

A voice said, "you are who you are supposed to be."

Slipping Beneath the Influence

I want to feel okay again.

I want to slip beneath the influence,

under the rock.

I beg you, don't turn it over...

because what you will find is dangerous and contagious.

I will infect you, be your best lover;

also, leave you in the dark and helpless.

You asked me what my flaws are.

I am flawed completely.

How much can you take?

I can take it all

but few can handle this crash.

I am a nightmare you can't wake up from,

a dream that you may regret.

I want to feel okay, so I slip beneath the influence.

I know you love me, but you will be crushed by this Granite,

and I am unapologetic about the impact.

Death

Death...
It's a lonely process.
Even with a thousand people around, you are alone.
Left, trapped in your mind.
By this point, the pain doesn't even matter.
Nothing can lift you up;
you know it's the end.
People care to a point,
but everyone has their own life to live.
Whether it's birth, the middle, or the lights going dim,
in the end, life and death are all we have;
life starts alone and ends alone.

Mi Ángel Guardián

It's all over now.

I've neglected my person for too long,

leaving behind the people who deserve my love and depend on it.

"What will they do without me," is the only thought on my mind.

I've been selfish, locking myself away from the world.

I feel so fucking alone but that doesn't matter, soon I'll be gone.

The Angel of Death is in front of me.

She is beautiful, all dressed in black.

Her touch is soft, but I know why she is here.

Fear is not the emotion that comes to mind, just loss;

the loss of what could have been,

and more so, what should have been.

The urge to fly with her is too tempting,

so I take her hand, and off we go.

I decided to give everything to her.

Where she takes me is dark, but her touch is still comforting.

I do see a spark in the distance.

That small light, I know can be a new dawn.

I've been here before,

but not like this.

She is different from the last time we've meant,

distracted and sad.

She is the only Person I can think about.

The Angel cries, and I take her hand.

"Come with me, you don't have to go through this in solitude.

Please come with me."

THANK YOU

Liv, you have done so much for me since we became friends. I can never repay the debt I owe you. I know you would never accept a payment, but I wish I could do for you what you have done for me. As of the time of making this book, this last year has been an experience.

You are a true friend and I love you.

Thanks, Liv.

Lighthouse

You are a beacon, something everyone is seeking,
a lighthouse to which broken and sinking ships sail toward.
Most of them crash ashore, never to be repaired.
They may never float again.
So many of us sink to the bottom, but your light is always shining.
A bright flame that never burns out.
It's a place many of us need to be.
Our compass always seems to point your way.
Even through the thickest fog, the worst storm, and folding waves,
even taken beneath by life's undertow, we always see that light.
Thank you for continuing to guide us to shore,
so we are not lost forever.

GANG!

Gang!

This is the first, but I cum with seconds;
I hear the call when the vagina beckons.
I hope you're hungry, I'm never empty,
my pen is filling, and I have plenty.
I just bust a load of ink on a page;
this book was pierced with a heavy gauge.
But the next will be light, to remedy your day,
with fits of laughter and totally gay.
Gang! - A Book with Words and Shit

LIST OF POEMS